DANCING WITH
GOD

A Spiritual Autobiography

DANCING WITH
GOD
A Spiritual Autobiography

Reverend Bobbie McKay, Ph.D.

iUniverse LLC
Bloomington

DANCING WITH GOD
A Spiritual Autobiography

iUniverse books may be ordered through booksellers or by contacting:

iUniverse LLC
1663 Liberty Drive
Bloomington, IN 47403
www.iuniverse.com
1-800-Authors (1-800-288-4677)

ISBN: 978-1-4917-1007-4 (sc)
ISBN: 978-1-4917-1008-1 (e)

Library of Congress Control Number: 2013918338

Printed in the United States of America.

iUniverse rev. date: 09/30/2013

CONTENTS

Contents v
About This Book xiii
Prologue xv

PART I
In The Beginning
Chapter 1.   Introduction 1
Chapter 2.   God Becomes Real In My Life 7
Chapter 3.   God And A Friend 10
Chapter 4.   God And The Piano 13
Chapter 5.   God In A "No"! 17
Chapter 6.   God In A "Yes"! 21
Chapter 7.   God In Action 24

PART II
God Can Do Anything
Chapter 8.   Meeting God Without Words 31
Chapter 9.   Five New Friends 34
Chapter 10.   Ministry Before The Electronic Church .. 37
Chapter 11.   A Traveling Church 40
Chapter 12.   God In Four Persons 42
Chapter 13.   When God Speaks Mountains Move 45
Chapter 14.   And The Doors Wouldn't Close 48
Chapter 15.   A Story About Bethlehem 51
Chapter 16.   Paul's Story 53
Chapter 17.   The Winds Of Change Arrive 56

PART III
I Thank You God, You're Breathtaking!

Chapter 18. God In Two Questions 63
Chapter 19. God On Highway 95 67
Chapter 20. Two Years On The Road With God 70
Chapter 21. Three Waitresses, One Artist And A Woman
In A Mental Hospital...78
Chapter 22. The Protestants Are Coming! 85
Chapter 23. Why Are You Discriminating Against
The Episcopal Church? 90
Chapter 24. God And The Internet...93
Chapter 25. God In The Army & Navy 95
Chapter 26. God And Our Questionnaires......................................99
Chapter 27. God, The Parish Nurses And George Gallup, Jr. 104
Chapter 28. God And The Librarian 107
Chapter 29. Making A New Christian Science Connection.......... 112
Chapter 30. On God And Harvard 115
Chapter 31. God At A Baseball Game... 118
Chapter 32. God In Four Books 125
Chapter 33. God In A Secretary's Mistake...................................128
Chapter 34. An Unexpected Visual Of God..................................136

PART IV
God Everywhere

Chapter 35. God In The Neighborhood 141
Chapter 36. God In Small Moments...145
Chapter 37. God In Another Parking Lot....................................... 151
Chapter 38. God And The "Boomers" 156
Chapter 39. God Never Leaves Loose Ends. 160
Chapter 40. God Is Not A Causal Agent..163
Chapter 41. God In Two "Miracles" 168
Chapter 42. A Different Kind Of "Miracle" 174
Chapter 43. God And Love...177
Chapter 44. God And Lew 182
Chapter 45. Dancing With God 186
Chapter 46. The Final Dance 190
Chapter 47. On Prayer, Gratitude And Endings 193

PART V

Afterward: Special Resources—Special Friends—Special Programs

Synopsis of Research Projects and Programs 201

Books and Publications 203

Author's Credentials 205

"Taking A Chance On God" Reverend Bobbie McKay, Ph.D.
and Lew Musil MFA 207

The Religious Experience Research Centre
WestMinster College, Oxford UK 209

Center for the Study Of World Religions
Harvard University 210

Review of "Healing the Spirit Stories of Transformation" 211

Reverend Dr. Fred Fourie, Pastor, Cocoa Beach
Community Church 213

The Reverend Jay Sidebotham, Rector,
The Church of the Holy Spirit, ... 214

The Reverend Gilbert W. Bowen, Retired Pastor 214

John Shea, Author, Lecturer, Story Teller 215

Reverend Gregory Sakowicz
Catholic Archdiocese of Chicago, IL 215

Rabbi Douglas Kohn San Bernardino, Ca. 215

The Reverend Paul Sherry, Ph.D., Former President,
United Church of Christ. 216

Reverend Elizabeth Andrews Presbyterian Minister
and Spiritual Director 216

The Reverend Wendy Lane, Retired Episcopal Priest 216

T. Tolbert Chisum, Businessman and Philanthropist 217

The Reverend Jane Fisler Hoffman,
Former Illoinois Conference Minister Of The United Church
Of Christ 217

Excerpts from "The Spiritual Healing Project Goes to School",
The Christian Science Sentinel, September 12, 2004. 217

Student Evaluations for Courses Taught at
Chicago theological Seminary 219

God And The Spiritual Life Teams 221

God And The Interfaith Dialogue Program 223

"Many Faces" An Interspiritual-Program For Adolescents
& Young Adults.. 225
George Gallup, Jr. and Dr. Bobbie McKay, Princeton,
New Jersey, 2011 227

For God who is Always
Waiting to Dance

Special Thanks to Lew,

Who is always there;

My children and my grandchildren;

And to all the people who have entrusted me

With their God experiences; shared their spiritual lives;

Prayed and cried with me.

God has blessed us with Presence and Love,

New Life and Energy; Peace and Joy;

And vast amounts of Laughter.

With Love,

Bobbie

ABOUT THIS BOOK

Dancing with God may be thought of as a "Digital Book" which is like a computer program in which the stories are arranged in a way to give you important information.

Each of the more than fifty God stories which appear in the book might be considered a "bit" of information which can be read in multiple ways: in the order in which the stories appear; by your design of choosing the order of the stories; by relying upon randomness; or perhaps by that which is God's design for you.

May you find your own God stories within these pages to help enrich your spiritual life.

Dancing with God is also a powerful way to share God experiences in a group setting.

PROLOGUE

This is a book about God: this force for life; this indescribable energy; this glorious light that is never extinguished. This is the same God that also lives in intimate connection with each one of us; who never leaves us, but who also waits for us to discover what life with God is all about.

This book is the story of the entrance of God in my life. Like a spiritual tsunami that transforms everything in its path, God walked into my world, transformed my life and has never left.

For the past nearly fifty years, I have been privileged to listen to thousands of people sharing their experiences with God. I have learned from all of them that God's signature is always a changed *new life*: not material gain or good fortune; not an uncluttered life; not a problem free existence. Instead, we discover an unexpected, cherished life with God as partner, creating a life-long passionate process of discovery and energy.

This book is organized according to the path I've followed with God from the first day God entered into my life to the present day of writing this book. I was living an ordinary life as a wife and mother with a conscious agenda that didn't include any plans with God, when God disrupted my organized existence and changed everything.

Today as a psychologist, ordained minister, researcher, writer and composer, I know that none of this would have happened without God's interventions in my life.

This dynamic, ever-present God is always available, but not according to our plans and schedules. Our preconceived ideas of God are entirely lost in the reality of meeting God face to face, moment to moment. Too often we've sanitized God to be devoid of passion and majesty. But the God I've come to know is paradoxically both power and intimacy, a catalytic force that explodes with creative energy and excitement, in which results are less important than the journey taken.

This book is for anyone who wants to know more about this intimate, personal God who resides within each of us. Familiar words describe the process of learning about God with great truth and simplicity: "I once was blind, but now I can see!" And what I see is God everywhere.

A few rules on the road to discovering God in our lives:

> We don't find God; God finds us.
> We can't see God except through other people.
> We don't know God's "plan" except as new life becomes the anchor of the outcome.

The one truth I have learned about life is that God is always present and I drift in and out of the relationship. God is the constant. I am the wanderer. My continuous prayer is to stay connected and to love God as deeply as God has unexpectedly loved me.

Now in my eighties, I see God's appearances in my life as unexpected connections with other people; moments of insight and understanding; loving moments that defy words; painful lessons learned; surprising opportunities that were clearly gifts from God; moments when God became so real that to identify them as anything but God would be to deny the presence of God in my life and in the world.

God appears in the best of times and the worst of times; in a flash of recognition or a slow arrival of understanding. God is always with us and sometimes we *get* it as quickly as it happens. Other times, we are ponderously slow in catching on. Most of the time we forget that God is right here, right now and we remain lost in a state of spiritual blindness and emptiness.

Then this God of all love and presence touches us in the gentlest of ways, or in a hail storm of reality, and we remember: *God is mystery; God is presence. We live in the intersection of two realities: When mystery becomes presence, God becomes real.*

This book is a collection of moments when God became real in my life. All of them were unexpected gifts that transformed my life. I didn't seek them nor try to organize or control them. God simply entered the moment and, if I were choosing to pay attention, there was no question that God was in the neighborhood just waiting for my response.

When I was wise enough to respond, the world opened in unexpected new ways that were never a part of my life plan, but which were designed to grow my spirit exponentially. Once I recognized the gift of God in my life, these new opportunities became the footprints of this entirely unexpected God who was now in charge of my life.

God challenges us to follow a new pathway; to trust that Love does not abandon us; and that Spirit-linked to Spirit will change the world.

I've organized these God experiences as moments experienced in my personal life; in my life as a pastor and psychologist; and in the world around me which is where God is always to be found. I've included several stories that involved my husband, Lew Musil, who accompanied me on this journey from the very beginning. I hope you can use these God moments as a catalyst to discover God in your life. It will set you on a mission that is beyond description.

You won't find any explanations of God in this book. No one can explain God. But God appears in everyone's life at some time through an experience in which God becomes visible through other people; through our senses; or through our heart and spirit which long for connection. God is an in-your-life force engaged in a lost and found operation directed into the world. When we have been *found*, we are entirely changed by this power of love calling us into relationship.

For each of us, life is the medium. But God is the message. This book is an invitation for you to make the same discovery in your life.

One hint may be helpful. God's *other* name is always "surprise"!

PART I

IN THE BEGINNING

"IN THE BEGINNING WAS THE WORD
AND THE WORD WAS WITH GOD
AND THE WORD WAS GOD."

Prologue to the Gospel of John

CHAPTER I

Introduction

*When does God begin in our lives? When are we aware of God
in our lives? What is the "switch" that turns on
our God connection?*

Many of us go through life with a picture of God that's something like our first interactions with our early caretakers. Like a spiritual conduit, they show us the parameters of existence and they coax us into life with the reality of their care: heart to heart; body to body; spirit to spirit. Our transition into the world is complete and the experience is stored somewhere in our spirit as our first internal awareness of what God *might* be like.

The trouble is that some care takers aren't able to love us very well; or their love is mixed with fear and anger or, sometimes, they are so filled with their own survival needs, our needs are simply too much. When that happens, our first experiences of the *God of safe-care* become an ambivalent message of confused signals. Sometimes we are greeted with delight; another time we are shunned or disregarded. Unable to understand the difference, we experience an emptiness we don't know how to fill.

These early non-verbal experiences of Spirit infuse us with the reality of connection. We are not alone! Or they confuse us when the messenger is neither reliable nor constant and we are left to live in the dark of not knowing what will happen next. In either case, they are stored somewhere in our memory bank to be examined later when our quest to know who God is in our life becomes more urgent and necessary to our spiritual growth.

In my life, my parents were instrumental in my early physical survival. At five weeks of age, I contracted pneumonia at a time when the powerful drugs of today were non-existent. My only hope of living was thought to be in the sunshine and warmth of Florida where this newborn body might heal. My parents and God became intertwined as partners in my struggle to live and God and life prevailed. In some inner spirit place, in an unspoken language, I experienced God as a source of *healing* in my life.

Two years later, my parents became change agents in the growth of my spirit. They would never have labeled their behavior as *God-connected*. But they had a conviction that children needed to be taught special skills unavailable in the public school environment. I was given piano lessons in my second year of life. And, most important, I was handed over to a dancing teacher at three years of age to learn how to dance. They chose a woman who trained children to dance on the stage, not simply to dance for fun and amusement. Dancing became embedded in my being *and* a profession.

In this amazing environment of sound, rhythm and movement, my spirit burst into life.

My dancing teacher would not have recognized God in the work she was doing. But she knew how to recognize a spirit that was being fed through her instructions, and I discovered a rhythm and force for life that would become a permanent part of who I was. God was still unspoken and unnamed, but God was filling me with spirit and life.

A few years later, two other people would continue my spirit-birthing process without ever speaking of God. The first was a woman who taught me you can "sing" without having a voice, so long as you are willing to work at it. A voice with spirit will always be heard. The second was a teacher who taught me that girls have the ability to do anything that attracts them, if they use their brains. Both messages became permanent God gifts for my spirit. I would not yet have my own language for "spirit". But I would know and recognize the results!

Generally, young children are exposed to a kind of Sunday school idea of God whether they attend a religious community or not. This God is usually powerful, distant, wise and reliable so long as we respond with appropriate diligence and obedience. This God offers a quid pro quo partnership: you do what is right and God will be around to protect you. God is a super *parent* who teaches us the rules of living and trains us for life.

Later, powerful stories of women and men in the Bible or the Koran or other spiritual resources will teach us about people who have already encountered God. If we are part of a religious community, we may learn special prayers and rituals to celebrate God's constancy and faithfulness.

Whatever our religious background or understanding of the nature of God, sometime in our adulthood we come to a spiritual crossroads where we need to learn a critical lesson about God. God must now move beyond our internalized parental figures (good or bad) to enter into a personalized relationship with us: not as a magical and special friend who will grant our wishes and attend to our needs; or a punishing parent who shapes our behavior with a special series of rewards or punishments.

But the God of all time and space who is as *real* as the next breath we take.

By this time in our growth process, we've already found the *magical God* to be lacking in multiple situations in which God didn't give us what we wanted or thought should happen. It's no wonder that so many of our young adults have left their religious roots because they find no usefulness in a God who doesn't enter into life to make it better. Why believe in that which is no longer believable or helpful? Instead, they choose to look for some spiritual experience which has enough personal empowerment to satisfy their needs for a better life and their hopes for a safer world.

What has been lost in today's world is the reality of what God actually is for all people, regardless of religious, economic, geographic or personal orientation. In fact, God may not always *save* us or *heal* us or make us feel *better at all.* If you use the Christian experience as an example, even Jesus cried out to God, "Why have you abandoned me?" before that question was fully answered in his resurrection.

The reality we must understand is that God's promise is God's Presence in our moment-to-moment daily lives. The constancy of that promise is told in the lives of millions of people who have *experienced* God and whose lives have been transformed by their God experiences.*

The God I learned about through others who nurtured and fed my spirit must now become the God I can recognize in my own life: *the God who resides with me, in me, and through me.*

For most of us, this process of knowing God is preceded by an undefined time in the darkness of not knowing, while seemingly disconnected events move us toward a moment of awareness: a sudden understanding of who God really is and a connection to God that defies logic, planning or any human endeavor to make God real.

In fact, God becomes *real* in our lives when we least expect it to happen; when it's inconvenient, out of the blue and entirely out of our control. The reality of God is seen in a transformed life alive with Spirit. The choice is always ours. Say *Yes* to God and New Life begins. Say *No* to God and God waits for the next time.

New life is the critical language of the God experience. It is the measurement of God's presence. For some the appropriate word is *transformation* which means that God has become real.

However, there is a price-tag for the gift of God. That price is our life. Once we accept the gift of God/Spirit in our life, we have an obligation to pass the gift to others by sharing our God experiences. Our relationship with God is an active partnership of love received and love given. It is our responsibility to pass it on.

What about your life? When did you become aware of God's presence in your life? Did anyone talk to you about God? Do you remember when you first encountered your own spirit?

If you're not yet aware of God in your life—or if you haven't yet discovered your own Spirit as a manifestation of God in you—then pay attention to what happens within you as you read through the God experiences in this book. Our experiences will differ, but circumstances in other lives may help you recognize a God experience you've already had.

One caution! Do not expect this to be an easy, comfortable process. (Think ultimate roller coaster!) God does not prevent life from impinging on us in multiple, often uncomfortable ways. But God does not abandon us in the middle of the mess either.

Each time we look past our current crisis and discover the new life that God is offering us, our spirit expands. Every moment we recognize God, in the midst of whatever issues we are facing, our spirit becomes stronger. And when we discover that God is always with us, our spirit transcends all limitations and restrictions and discovers the richness and constancy of God.

But remember! God isn't a Santa Claus character that provides us with presents. God isn't directing our lives like chess players on a board. God is not trouble-free. God is offering us new spiritual life that moves us into a God-Space of possibilities and open doors, *unexpected grace* and *amazing love.*

That gift triumphs over all others.

So get ready, pack your bags and get ready for your new life to begin!

God operates on a 24/7 plan so the moment could be right now! Take a chance and start looking at your life as if God were your constant companion. That means you are not alone. God is right now and God is forever! In between those two states are multiple opportunities to discover God in your life through experiences with others or moments when God simply enters your heart and becomes *real.*

This book will open the door to the God I've experienced in my own life and invite you to discover God in yours. Set aside all preconceived ideas about God and let these shared experiences speak directly to your heart and spirit. God will do the rest!

---

*   In Part V, the "Afterward" section of this book, I have described the research studies we conducted to learn about people's experiences of God in their lives. Their stories plus my own experiences of God represent profound evidence of the constancy of God in life. There is no question that God is a reality in ordinary life that is ever present, accessible and life giving for all people, regardless of what we bring to the table of life.

Statements from people who have been involved with our research studies and subsequent programs are also included.

Our research appears in three other published books, available at Amazon. com.

Bobbie McKay and Lewis A. Musil, *Healing the Spirit: Stories of Transformation* (Allen, Texas: Thomas More Publications, 2000).

Bobbie McKay and Lewis A. Musil, *Taking a Chance on God: Exploring God's Presence in our Lives* (iUniverse, 2007) with Forward by George Gallup, Jr.

Bobbie McKay, *When God Becomes Real: Stories of Presence, Models of Church* (Exploration Press, 2008).

The research study also appears in: *Religion and Healing in America*", Susan Sered and Linda Barnes. (Oxford University Press, 2004).

CHAPTER 2

God Becomes Real In My Life

*How does God become real in our lives? What opens the door
for the entrance of the Living God into our Heart and Spirit?*

Before God became *real* in my life, I was already married with three children. As far as I knew, God was a permanent resident in the church on Sunday mornings *only*. Or so I thought. But God does not play life safely in the confines of a building. God emboldens the world to act and life always shifts before we may be ready for the change. I thought I already knew all about God through the people who had grown my spirit. But that was only a kindergarten step in my spiritual journey.

We were attending a neighborhood Episcopal Church where our children were enrolled in the Sunday school program. Unfortunately, the program spoke of a God who watched the children's every move, ready to pounce and punish if transgressions called for such judgments. That didn't fit my limited idea of God at all. Surrounding myself with a mantle of courage, I complained to the priest in charge about the God messages being given to my children. His response was swift and final. I was asked to leave my church home and seek God elsewhere! I was no longer welcome in the church.

My response to being judged and dismissed surprised me. I was overwhelmed with grief and loss and felt inconsolable. It was as if something had died in me. Where would I find God if I couldn't find God in the church? Where was God anyway? Like an abandoned child, I looked for God everywhere and found nothing.

But in my state of feeling profoundly *lost,* a neighbor just happened to invite me to join the choir at his Methodist church. The familiar door of music began to engage my spirit. God may or may not have been in the Methodist church. But remembrances of God/Spirit/Music began to stir my heart.

And then one day—a day when I wasn't thinking about God at all—God appeared in my dining room: God in *my* world; God in *my* heart and spirit; God in a single moment; and my life was changed forever, in a millisecond of time.

It was not a spiritual setting nor was I engaged in anything remotely considered *spiritual* I was cleaning the bookcase in the dining room the way my mother taught me to clean: methodical, thorough and entirely thoughtless. I took each book off the shelf: dusted the front and back covers, cleaned along the binding in all directions, dusted the space on the shelf where the book belonged, and returned the book to its cleaned space.

Repetitiously, I continued the process while my mind became a blank page: no thoughts, only the sense of a task that needed to be accomplished properly. The children were at school. Our dog was fast asleep in the sunshine flooded dining room. Life was quiet, fully contained in this smooth operation of books and space until I reached for my copy of the Bible which was just as dusty as all the other books had been. (I was a church goer, not a Bible reader.)

For unknown reasons, I paused in my designated process, put down my dusting equipment, noted the cover and opened the book. But I didn't turn to the first page. I simply opened the Bible to whatever place *it chose* to open which turned out to be the Prologue to the Gospel of John.

And I read the prologue out loud to an unseen audience:

> *"In the Beginning was the Word, and the Word was with God and the Word was God".*

As if I needed to hear the message again, I read the words out loud a second time:

> *"In the Beginning was the Word, and the Word was with God and the Word was God."*

To ensure that I heard this message, unseen forces called me to read it aloud one more time.

> *"In the Beginning was the Word, and the Word was with God and the Word was God".*

With this third reading, my world shifted. It was the only way I could describe the experience. It felt like the sudden opening of a door I didn't even know existed. Enter an invisible, but *recognizable in my spirit God*, and my life changed in an instant of time. Without questioning, I knew this was God entering my life. Without thinking, I was suddenly engulfed in the presence of God and the dining room filled with Spirit. Without knowing, I understood that God had become *real* in my world and my life changed forever.

Somehow, I also learned that my life now belonged to God. Whatever that meant, it was a statement of truth received and life transformed: a new beginning of everything. I had been lost in the pain of separation from the church. But I had also clearly and undeniably been found by God.

The God who had not saved me from the awful wrench of separation and loss from the church was the same God who entered my life in the place where I lived. Both experiences were necessary for me to know who God is and the reality and permanency of my God connection. *This was a God I could trust with my life.*

God is right now, a permanent part of the world. *God becomes real* whenever we learn to recognize the God who resides in the center of our lives. *God is New Life* if we are willing to engage in the relationship.

It really is that simple!

CHAPTER 3

God And A Friend

*What happens when someone else
doesn't see the "light" you discovered?*

After my experience with God in my dining room, I was so filled with spirit that I wanted to tell someone what had happened. Believing it would actually be possible to describe my experience, I picked up the phone to call a close friend. I couldn't wait to share it!

The words came flying out of my heart and spirit with no restrictions as to content or delivery. I tried to explain the essence of the experience in a few words. But my heart wouldn't let me shortchange the reality of God in my life. I blurted it all out in a way that must have seemed a little crazy at worst, and pretty strange at best.

The avalanche of words ended with a short statement to summarize the entire experience. "I don't know what this means but I know it has changed my life." I took a deep breath, sighed with the enormity of the experience and waited. A long moment of silence came from the other end of the line.

And then my friend filled the silence with words I wasn't expecting to hear. "Well gotta go!" she exclaimed brightly and hung up the phone.

I was surprised and . . . I was not surprised. I was outwardly silent, but inwardly examining what had just happened. I sat for a moment, taking in the room, re-experiencing everything that had happened. I felt a strange state of *nothingness* followed by a powerful and extraordinary sense of God's Presence.

With great care and attention to all remembered details, I went through the entire experience, including the finale with my friend. I found myself both thanking God and knowing that everything that had happened on that day was true.

I knew I had been in the presence of God. The words from the prologue to the Gospel of John would always be the signal for me to know all I needed to know about God. From the beginning of all time and space, there is God. From the beginning of life, there is always God. From this new beginning in my life, God had now become the center and anchor of everything.

My friend's reaction was a powerful lesson I needed to learn about God in the world. It would not be the last time that someone would question my convictions and experience. It would not be the last time that someone would think I was some kind of crazy religious person. It would not be the last time that my knowing God would cost me a relationship.

Not everyone will see God as I have. Not everyone will want to know God as I do. Not everyone will be willing to engage in a conversation about God. It is better to know this in advance. It is far better to be prepared for rejection, disregard and distance.

I never saw my friend again. What I had experienced was not where she needed to be. Curiously, the cost was not high because the reward for knowing God was beyond words and descriptions. Later I understood it was my responsibility to pray that someday she might know God in her life. After that, the loss simply passed from my consciousness.

Once again, God had given me a double gift: the gift of presence and the gift of wisdom to know that there will always be a voice of rejection and disbelief when God becomes manifest. Some will see; many will not. All may want to experience God. But the gate is narrow and the path demands a commitment without qualifications.

In knowing God, I had begun my new life. I was a newborn in this new journey to recognize and acknowledge God in my life. But this time, I had a profound understanding that God was already and permanently there.

It would always prove to be more than sufficient.

Praise God for all the Yes's and the No's that shape us and guide us through the maze we live in called *life*. In profound thanks for the constancy of God's Presence and Love. Amen.

CHAPTER 4

God And The Piano

*What happens when you do something
you can't explain?*

Within a few weeks of my God discovery in my dining room, I was invited to a neighborhood coffee. Being new in the area, this seemed a good opportunity to meet people. I looked forward to the occasion, anticipating a pleasant experience and some new friends.

Since my friend's recent rejection of my encounter with God, I had not attempted to share my God experience with anyone. I kept it in my heart and spirit, frequently turning it over in my mind as a precious gift that needed no words or explanations. The repetition of memory only added to its value. But I had no idea of the scope of things to come as a result of my meeting with God.

On a quiet, uneventful day in early summer, I walked to my neighbor's house and rang the doorbell, without thinking about God at all. A man answered the door. Curiously, he didn't invite me in nor say any words of greeting. Instead he started the conversation as if we had already been talking for several moments. I had to concentrate on listening because his words didn't make any sense.

"I have two pianos," were his first words, followed by, "one is a baby grand and the other is a large upright. The small grand piano is in the living room and the upright is in the hall near the dining room." He paused for a moment allowing me enough time to look behind me to see who he was talking to. It couldn't have been me. But there was no one there and I had never met this man before.

He continued in the same friendly, informative way. "I think you'd do better with the upright. It's a wonderful piano and has a marvelous tone. On the other hand, if you'd really prefer the baby grand, you'll have an instrument that will be very satisfying", or words to that effect. The conversation was difficult to follow because it had no basis in reality as far as I was concerned.

For unknown reasons, I decided to go along with this stream of information. In a rather manufactured, but friendly way, I asked, "How much is the upright?" all the time wondering why I was having this unusual conversation with a stranger. He seemed pleased that I was "choosing" the upright. "It's $75. You'll really enjoy this instrument. It's a very special piano."

Surprisingly, my mind began to calculate how I could pay $75 for this unwanted piano. It was not because he was so persuasive. I simply was not in the market to buy a piano and I couldn't afford $75 for anything. I'd had piano lessons as a young two to five year old, but had been deemed unworthy of lessons at age six because of limited talent. In fact, I had not touched a piano in over twenty five years. But something was happening in this encounter that made it necessary for me to respond to this strange and unexpected transaction.

With newly discovered conviction that made no sense to me, still standing outside the door, I found myself saying, "OK! I'll buy the upright; I'll pay you $5 per month until it's paid for. You'll pay for the moving". He smiled, shook my hand and closed the door. I never went in.

Sight unseen, I had bought a piano I didn't want. I never played it to see what it sounded like. It didn't occur to me to find out about the inner mechanics of the instrument. I simply said, "Yes" to a stranger who was offering me something I never intended to buy.

Walking home, I was in a curious state of non-being. I announced to the family that I had bought a piano which would arrive at our house in about a week. No one seemed surprised at all.

In planning the future location of the piano in our home, the dining room was the first and best choice. In older homes, the dining room was often as large as the living room, giving it a spacious and quiet quality that invited *spirit* in for conversation and life. It was also the place of nourishment.

After the first rush of excitement when the piano was delivered, I brought a chair over, sat down in front of it and touched the keys. It *did* have a wonderful tone. It had been so many years since I'd played a piano that nothing came to mind to play. But the piano had clearly been well cared for and kept in good tune.

Its placement in the dining room, on an inside wall for protection from the outside elements, separated from the noise and activity of the kitchen was exactly right. The piano seemed comfortable and at home. It was enough for one day.

Within a few days, I began to hear original melodies that came from some unknown place in my brain. Without a repertoire to remember, my spirit seemed to be supplying a combination of musical sounds and words that became individual songs. I began to recognize God's actions in this unfolding story of the piano that had come to live at our house.

God was still so new in my life that I didn't immediately think *"God"* when this surprising experience took place. One part of me had only known that the piano was something I *had* to buy. But *why* and *what for* were unanswered questions until I actually started to play the piano. Then the skills that had been found lacking when I was six years old, dormant for so many years, suddenly took shape and form in my thirty two year old being.

Within a few months, I volunteered to write a musical for the 90th anniversary of the Methodist Church I was now attending. Six months later, the musical was performed at the church and the 90th anniversary was accomplished. According to the trustees of the church, the musical was the biggest and most successful event the church had ever experienced. Music and words were flowing from an inner source that grew more audible every day.

The piano reacquainted me with the power of music to fill life with harmony and pleasure. It can transport us to unexpected places where the heart expands to new levels of knowing. In its *word-less-ness*, music always speaks directly to our spirit.

My piano was my first actual God gift—a gift I would never have bought for myself, yet it was mine for the taking. And it transformed my entire life. I still tell myself the story of my piano whenever I need to be reminded of the power and breadth of God in the world. It was as if those early years of piano and dance grew silently and internally until the right moment came when they could fill my life with the miracle of words and music.

My spirit now had a full range of expression that it had never experienced before. I had lived in such a *silent* world. Now I had a language of connection.

Who could have predicted that one piano would become a life-long expression of spirit for me? Its never ending, creative possibilities are breathtaking realities and indisputable evidence of the love and presence of God in the world. And, of course, the entire experience clearly established that God's other name is always *surprise!*

In your own life, is there something you do that allows your spirit free expression? Is there a time or place or activity that opens the door to the presence of God or Spirit in your life? Let you heart and spirit search for those moments when new life *interrupts* your normal, everyday life and shifts your energy into a new direction.

That's what God is all about! We don't plan God's moves in life. If *we* had that power, life would be far less interesting than life with God in charge!

CHAPTER 5

God In A "No"!

*What Happens When You Suddenly
Find Yourself in New Place?*

So far, God and I were batting a thousand! Everything was working well. Music flowed; life was an unfolding surprise. But it wasn't long before unexpected, new intimations of change slipped into my spirit, hints of things to come. I was casually receptive but not very attentive until the theme of these changes began to become very clear. It was not what I expected.

"Ministry? Me? No, I don't think so." It was 1966. "Women don't go into ministry. They go into teaching or nursing. Ok, even Christian Education. Not ministry."

But my spirit would not be put to sleep. It continued to speak in a gentle, but firm voice, whispering ideas about God that were never a part of my life plan.

"No! I'm not interested. I don't see myself as a minister." Still the thoughts wouldn't leave. My spirit was relentless in its pursuit of this newly discovered, thoroughly unexpected goal.

"No! That's crazy. Enough already!"

"Go away! I'm not listening."

Then I met with the Christian Education Director of my Methodist church and trusted my unexpressed heart into her welcoming spirit.

"I think I want to go into the ministry. I know it's crazy. It feels right". And she smiled and said "Go for it!"

However, there remained two imposing variables. The minister of this Methodist church had to approve my request to go to seminary. And the local seminary had to accept my application. Both were nearly out of question. It was too soon; women weren't welcome in churches or seminaries; change was coming. But not yet!

But then there was God. And God was leading all of us out of the wilderness toward the *promised land*.

First came the minister. Tall, southern, imposing, eloquent, judgmental, thoroughly Methodist, and very firm!

"No", he said when I approached him with the idea of my going into the ministry. "It's not a good idea". He paused in the shuffling of papers on his desk, avoiding eye contact at all costs, and seemed to be thinking out loud about the reality of my situation.

"Women don't belong in the ministry." He paused for a moment of clarification. "You belong at home with your husband and your children. This is not a profession for women. You can't give enough time to it and you don't have any experience with what it takes to minister to a congregation. No. It definitely won't work".

Fortunately I was wise enough to keep quiet while this challenge to the ordained ministry from a woman entered the room and didn't go away. A long silence followed, more paper shuffling and no eye contact.

The silence was finally broken with his closing argument. "No, I will not support this idea of yours to go into the ministry. That's final". Like a judge in a court of misdemeanors, he now had full control of the situation and declared his opinion on the matter at hand.

I didn't say a word. But my silence was not empty. God was there and we were getting very close to the *promised land!*

Suddenly he shifted in his posture and attitude. And he looked directly at me, taking in the reality of my presence and my request.

"OK! OK! I won't support you. I don't believe it's right. It isn't! That's where I stand. But if you can get the congregation to support you, I won't interfere!" A flick of his hand indicated our interview was over.

And somewhere God must have smiled because this was the church that had celebrated its 90th anniversary with the musical I had written, still actively remembered as the most successful and exciting event in their history.

How could they say "no"?

When approached, the local Methodist seminary said, "You have a year to prove you can do the work. If you do, and fulfill all our expectations and obligations, you're in."

We had reached *the promised land:* the place of new beginnings and new spirit.

Three years later, when I had finished my course work and was ready to graduate and be ordained into ministry in the Methodist Church, I returned to share the good news with the minister. We'd had no contact during those years. I knew the many changes of the 1960's had troubled him. It was not just women in the ministry. It was a time of revolution that reverberated throughout the lives of everyone. The church was no exception.

I walked into his office and saw the price of these changes in his face and posture. We shook hands silently. I took a seat and waited for him to begin.

Finally, I broke the silence. "I've finished seminary and will be ordained in two weeks". He nodded but didn't smile. Knowing that my silence was now entirely necessary, I waited for him to respond.

Suddenly, he got up from his chair, moved quickly across the room to the closet where his clerical robes were hung. He took out a white robe, brought it over to me and handed it into my arms. His words astonished me! "My grandfather wore this robe when he was ordained. My father and I both wore this robe when we were ordained. You take it and you wear it!"

Avoiding eye contact at all costs, he brushed past me toward the safety of his desk and quickly sat down.

I looked at the white robe in my lap—this extraordinary, unexpected symbol of past, present and future which now covered my entire body. Words were useless to describe the sacredness of this moment. I tried to express my truly heartfelt thanks for this profound gesture on his part. Not comfortable with my attempts, he simply nodded and turned to his paper work to change the subject.

But God's presence already filled the room. I had reached my destination and my journey into ministry had begun.

This God of surprising gifts always speaks directly to heart and spirit. When we respond to this invitation, our spirit finds a permanent home in God and waits for the next directions to appear.

God's next appearance would be in a brand new, entirely unexpected setting.

CHAPTER 6

God In A "Yes"!

When the unusual and unexpected happens,
God must be near.

With seminary training completed, the next step was unknown, but not for long. Thanks to a high school friend I hadn't seen in years, an opportunity arrived to apply for the Ph.D. program at Northwestern University in counseling psychology. God's signature of surprise was unmistakable.

I was accepted into the program immediately.

Included in that special academic package was the opportunity to train with and be supervised by a psychiatrist who taught in the post graduate program at the seminary. If I could manage, I could do both programs.

I was beginning to understand the depth of God's Presence and activity.

My psychiatrist supervisor was rather short in stature, quiet and soft spoken, a man of very few words. I rarely saw him laugh. He listened, looked for a teaching opportunity, and was always honest in his appraisal of my work with people. I learned to deeply value these moments of insight which I was privileged to receive.

In the two years we spent together as supervisor and supervisee, we never spoke of anything personal in either of our lives. He was my teacher; I was a student absorbing every word of understanding he offered as pure gift.

When the time came for me to complete my training, suddenly questions and doubts flooded my heart and spirit. "How do you really help people?" "What makes this healing process work?" "How will I ever be useful to others?" "What will I say to people?" "How will I know what to do?"

In our final meeting, my supervisor seemed to sense some of my dis-ease and my questions without my having to speak them out loud. Looking at me with great seriousness, he paused for a moment of silence and then spoke directly to my personal, soon to be professional, life. I expected to hear words that would ease my anxiety and restore my confidence. But the words he selected were a total surprise!

"Now *forget* everything you've learned," he began quietly, searching my face for my response. I couldn't believe my ears. Seeing my confusion, he repeated his words.

"Forget everything you've learned". That didn't make any sense to me at all. In my confusion, I could only repeat his words.

"Forget everything?" I protested, unwilling to reject all the knowledge and wisdom I had gained in seven years of graduate study. I couldn't yet *see* the unexpected gift I was being offered.

He paused to think about my response and added in a softer voice, "Forget everything and just be with people". But my mind was still trying to absorb his words. How could I possibly forget everything and still do the work I trained for?

He assumed a much gentler tone and manner, his words carrying a truth *he* knew I needed to hear.

"Yes, forget everything", he paused for a second or two, "and just be with people." And then he added words aimed directly at my heart.

"You have the gift. Now use it."

My heart listened carefully to those deeply personal words and *heard* them: "You have the gift. Now use it."

Everything in the room became quiet. Permission had been given and received. I spoke a silent prayer of gratitude.

In that single moment, my new life had been blessed and sanctified.

God always works through those who enter our lives to teach and prepare us for being God's agents in the world. Their presence shifts our world into a God center from which everything can flow. They train us to become the next generation of spiritual teachers.

With profound thanks for their presence and their gifts.

Amen.

CHAPTER 7

God In Action

When Life isn't how you planned it,
take a chance and say "yes"!

When looking at stories in most religious traditions, God gets top billing in any human adventure providing we're able to recognize and trust God's presence. It's the only way we can account for the mystery that pervades human life. We try to be in control of our lives and live them the way we think they should unfold. We do the right things and hope for the best.

But the moment God enters the scene, all bets are off. God is like a lightning rod that catapults us into the future with no time to plan or exercise our controls. God is all *yes* or *no!* Are you with me or against me? If you're with me, hang on for your life is about to change and there's no looking back for an exit door. If you're not yet ready, I'll be back.

I was now an ordained minister without a job, in an environment that was negative or ambivalent at best about women in the ministry. Where was God in that seemingly impossible situation?

And so it was that a new story began and a not so very still or small voice entered the world in the persons of a group of women who had a vision. Their vision was simple and direct: They wanted a woman minister to come to their church and form a ministry to women.

I needed a job. We lived in different communities. Somehow, we had to find each other. And that was entirely up to God.

I just happened to be interviewed by a local newspaper about my ordination. One of the questions raised by the reporter was how I felt about groups of women in the church, generally known as women's associations. What did I think about them? Emboldened by my recent graduation, I answered quickly: "I don't think they speak to the needs of women" and I suggested perhaps they ought to close their doors and find out what women really wanted. End of statement.

That inflammatory remark moved the article to the front page of the publication where the women who were searching for their own woman minister found the person they were looking for. The rest of the story is God in Action.

I began my ministry in a large, suburban church outside of Chicago. Everything that could go wrong did go wrong. Hiring a minister only for the women of the church meant I couldn't do ministry for the men of the church. The women, finding a minister outside the chain of command on their own, (without consulting the other clergy and the official governing body of the church) created a debacle of authority.

Being a woman minister in 1970 meant unleashing the whole issue of the women's rights and authority, crowned by one simple question: *If Jesus had really wanted a woman disciple, he would have chosen one!* (Issue closed forever!)

Divisions upon divisions were unleashed. The women were undaunted. Efforts to remove me were met with continuous support. The women (and a few men who had joined their ranks) were like evangelists so filled with spirit they could not be contained. The time had come and they were willing witnesses to a new spirit in the church.

Meanwhile, I was given a temporary office in a large second floor room in the church, about as far removed from the church offices as possible, with a wonderful exposure to the sunlight. The women furnished the room with a large couch, chairs, and a desk for me. It was suggested I meet with groups of women to increase my exposure in the church.

Seminary had not provided me with instructions for a small group ministry to women. But when I made it known I would be leading a group for women only, on a Tuesday morning, about a dozen women arrived precisely on time. And God and Spirit entered that sun-lit room and breathed light and life on all of us.

Without knowing what to do, I asked a simple question of the gathered group: "What's a word to describe what you are feeling right now?" The first words were tentative. I wrote each word on the blackboard provided in the room. Once those first words had been lovingly offered to the group, others poured out until the blackboard was covered with feeling words or phrases.

I looked at the women who had fearlessly assembled for our first group. We collectively looked at the words on our list and read them out loud together. It became our first prayer.

In nearly ten years of struggle, anguish and pain, God remained our constant. One by one, the issues of resistance were removed. One by one, people grew in spirit and truth. One by one, we came together as a loving community of God's Presence which grew to include both women and men.

To assuage those who were still in opposition, I was relegated to the room on the second floor and the basketball court in the basement. The second floor room became a healing place. The basketball court in the basement, where I led Sunday seminars, became a sanctuary where God's presence was continuous.

Communion in the basement under the basketball hoops was a sacred and life altering experience.

The Presence of God was unmistakable in the mountains of life, tears and laughter we shared.

And we came to believe, we learned to know that God might just have a sense of humor too.

In those upper and lower rooms, I learned to do ministry.

Meeting one-on-one or in small groups to heal life's pain on the second floor; being one and many in the basketball court in the basement where we learned how to live and love in the world. God in Life—God in our own personal worlds—God everywhere!

All of us learned to trust that God was real and present and that Love was essential in bringing new life into the church. We had overcome much of the resistance and grown into a community where everyone was welcome. I learned lessons about God never taught in seminary.

Seven years had passed since I had been hired by the women of the church to do ministry for the women of the church. We now had several groups of women looking at exciting and growing issues and opportunities for women. Groups of mothers talked about how to raise children. And the first group of men gathered to experience what the women were talking about. It was 1977 and God was alive in every moment.

A publisher contacted me to write a book about women. It became "The Unabridged Woman: A Guide to Growing Up Female", published in 1979. (Its original title was "The Unabridged Broad: A Guide to Growing Up Female", a much more descriptive title, but the publisher was afraid to go that far!)

I would stay in this amazing environment for nearly three more years. Opportunities kept arriving to bring more spirit into life and to discover the limitless nature of God. Change was everywhere and everything seemed possible . . . with God. It was a moment of *pause and relief*. Challenges had been confronted and withstood. We could all breathe a little more easily.

But the very edges of change were preparing their opening moves. You could feel it in wakeful moments in the night when sleep is disturbed, but the formless unknown is not quite ready to be revealed. My mind had no information about what was happening. But my spirit knew something was in the air.

I would learn that God's beginnings are often like that. It was time to pay attention and get ready, even in the dark!

Trusting God means trusting those life processes that move us toward new life when our thought processes aren't quite there yet! It's as if something in us initiates a new beat and energy before we know what that newness contains: a signal to keep our eyes and minds open to the unexpected thought, the unsolicited idea and the "this must be crazy" notion that comes at us, *seemingly* from nowhere.

When that happens, you can be sure that God is on the move again. And when God moves, new possibilities begin and life starts shifting like the waters that parted at the Red Sea, granting new freedom and new life!

Take a deep breath and fill your lungs with love and trust for the pending journey. Nothing in life is easy. But life with God is always NEW.

PART II

GOD CAN DO ANYTHING

"God can do anything, you know—
Far more than you could ever imagine or guess
In your wildest dreams!
God does it not by pushing us around,
But by working within us,
God's Spirit deeply and gently within us."

Ephesians 3:20-21
From the Message Bible

CHAPTER 8

Meeting God Without Words

When a friend really needs you and
you have no idea what to do . . .

His voice was desperate and angry. "You're a minister now. Well I need someone to minister to my wife. She's locked herself in our bedroom and won't open the door".

As I drove over to their home, all I could think about was how unprepared I felt to deal with his anger and whatever had happened to my friend. All I knew was that one of their children had recently been diagnosed with a brain tumor.

He was too frightened and angry to talk when I got there. Close to tears, he pointed upstairs and walked away. It was about 10:30 in the evening. I hurried up the stairs, caught my breath at the closed door, and knocked.

"Ann, it's me. Can I come in?" No response. My heart started to pound.

"Please let me come in?" The silence continued.

"Please, Ann." I didn't know what else to say. And from behind the door, a flat voice finally answered. "The door isn't locked."

I turned the knob quietly not knowing what I would find. The room was entirely dark, with the only light coming from the street light outside the window next to the bed. Ann was lying quietly in the bed, her eyes closed, a light blanket covering her body. No words were spoken by either of us.

I found a chair by the window and sat down. Something in me knew I could not be the one to break the silence.

I don't know how long we sat sharing the silence of this dark room. Finally, she said, "I'm blind".

The words carried a reality I could not question. Nor could I try to persuade her that she really wasn't blind. My internal censor told me to be still and wait.

The minutes began to accumulate in this room of silence. My heart knew that I could not interfere with whatever process was occurring. I was aware that my silence was critical for both of us.

After what seemed like several hours had passed, Ann spoke again: "I can't see anything". And I found myself saying, "I will not leave you".

I don't know where those words came from. Logic should have at least asserted itself to say, 'what if she really *is* blind? Shouldn't you be trying to persuade her to get medical help?'

But there was no logic in that room. Something going on in that darkened bedroom defied logic, easy answers or quick interventions.

The time continued to pass. It was as if we had entered a strange no-time zone. Finally, the early rays of dawn began to enter the room. I had been there the whole night. I walked to the side of the bed and sat down next to my friend. Her eyes were open. I reached for her hand. Looking at her, I knew the crisis of the night was over and so did she. It was time for me to leave.

"Shall I leave the door open?" I asked as I stood up. She nodded yes. I walked away in silence. But the silence was filled with the reality of what we had both experienced.

Ann and I never spoke about that evening. I understood the desperation she was feeling. "I can't see anything" meant I cannot look at the pain and fear I am experiencing over my son's brain tumor. I cannot look at it therefore I will not see anything.

And from deep inside some place of understanding, I knew the only words I could speak were the words of connection: "I will not leave you", with the assurance that my actions would speak that truth as well.

I didn't attempt to pray with her during that long night of silence. I knew God was in the room. I was aware of a powerful and wordless struggle to move beyond despair to some kind of hope. Words were not the answer.

Sometimes life is too much and we feel unable to withstand the pain.

Then the depth of God can be found in the *presence of God*: not to solve our pain-filled lives; not to make everything OK. Not to force us to change.

Just to be with us. Just to be there.

I learned the power of silence. I learned the reality of God's Presence. I learned the profound gift of love without words.

Solutions come when the time is ready, whether we feel prepared or not.

Amen.

CHAPTER 9

Five New Friends

My First Adventure in an Interfaith World

I first met this amazing quintet in 1976: Five women who decided they wanted to talk about God with my help. What made them so unusual were their religious affiliations. Two Jewish women, one Catholic woman and two Protestant women had somehow found each other and decided to search for God together. They invited me to share the journey.

Until this time, when people of different religious backgrounds got together it was usually a few Protestants and Catholics daring to approach each other with some curiosity and a lot of caution. You didn't want the religious orientation of the *other* to somehow rub off and become a contaminant in your own spiritual life. On the other hand, there was something exciting about engaging in these early ecumenical activities to explore our religious lives.

Sometimes, we went so far as to share some of our rituals with each other. Protestants might find a Catholic Church that permitted communion for non-Catholics on special occasions like weddings or funerals. Protestant and Catholic youth groups might share a community project. It was safe, and it allowed us to move past a few of our barriers without *challenging* our beliefs.

My group of five women courageously took the next step and included two Jewish women in their group. From the very beginning of our meetings, it felt amazingly and wonderfully right to blend Christians and Jews together in a dialogue about God. The time had arrived and we were ready to embark on a new journey of spiritual connections.

I never heard the full story of how they had found each other. They were friends of friends, all in their mid to late 30's. But God was clearly visible in the mix and I would soon discover that my time with this group would be a first step in my own journey to find God within the multi-diversity of many religious groups.

When adding representation from the Jewish community to the ecumenical experience of Protestants and Catholics, the result became an interfaith experience of Christians and Jews. No one spoke of adding an Islamic voice to the group at that time. Muslims lived on the other side of the world, or so we thought. This felt quite daring enough. My special quintet was at the cutting edge of an *inter-spiritual* world that was in its earliest stages of gestation.

Our time together was simple, exploratory, curious and accepting. We knew we were doing something quite special although it seemed quite ordinary at the same time. We were discovering our spiritual connections, but we rarely used the word "spiritual". We were listening and learning from each other and finding the process to be surprisingly easy.

We came to no brilliant conclusions. We didn't discover a powerful way to address our religious differences nor attempt a comparative study of our individual theologies. We simply came to be together and to honor the surprising gift we had been given. Each had a role to play in our awakening dialogue and each woman was essential to the experience.

When the time was right, the group stopped meeting. An inner and outer sense of discovery and satisfaction pervaded our final meeting. We had *heard* the call to explore the meaning of spiritual life among six women who were spirited novices living a wonderful new adventure.

At that final meeting, they presented me with an amazing gift: A special copy, signed by the author, of a limited edition book named, "*The Surrealist's Bible*". It contained an assortment of Biblical stories, described in words and powerful drawings by its author, Dierdre Luzwick. But the dedication in the book told the entire story of our group: "For our dear friend, Bobbie McKay, who helped us understand that God is Love."

In just a few months of time, we had discovered there were no spiritual differences between us. Without an agenda to explore, we experienced an anchor of trust and love that transcended our *religious* differences.

Twenty Five years later, I would be immersed in an interfaith study of Protestants, Catholics, Jews and Muslims. Our original group of five became an inter-spiritual community of over four thousand people who were discovering God everywhere.

But these five women were the beginning and the fulfillment of the promise: whenever two or three are gathered in God's name, God is present and blessings abound!

And God, as they discovered *and* experienced, is always Love.

CHAPTER 10

Ministry Before The Electronic Church

When clergy meet clergy and pray together.

In the 1970's, when the United Church of Christ was still young, and looking for its unique place in the church world, I was a recently ordained, Ph.D. psychologist with a passion for group ministry.

When the denomination decided to hold a leadership training weekend, I was called to plan and lead it. I had an entire day at my disposal, an unrestricted and generous gift.

The times were exciting and provocative. Coming out of the 50's and 60's, powerful changes had become the norm and God fit right into the excitement we were all feeling about this wonderful opportunity to discover and explore who we were as a church.

Nothing seemed too far to reach. Change was everywhere. Life was rich and full of possibilities. It was time to set aside our carefully constructed ideas of ministry; leave behind our lessons in theology and church management and explore a more intimate form of ministry with each other.

Since we were a comparatively young denomination, I had few precedents to shape the activities of the day. Because we were a more open and inclusive denomination, I decided we needed an opportunity to build *spiritual connections* without resorting to the usual psychological or social exercises. The total freedom I was given to choose and plan what we would do that day was a powerful and exciting gift.

I decided to bring the large gathered group together for four general informational sessions during the day and then divide them into smaller groups after each of the sessions to explore the message from the general sessions.

I would also train facilitators to meet with the smaller groups. I planned a sufficient break in between our four general sessions that I could meet for a few moments with our facilitators to answer any immediate questions or concerns they had in relation to their small group meetings.

My facilitators were either volunteers or selected because someone thought they'd do a good job. Carefully preparing leadership instructions for them, I kept the tasks low key and easy so that everyone would participate. This was not a day to divulge heart weary pain or heavy congregational problems or issues confronting the church.

What we needed to know was that we were part of something much larger than all of us and God was actively engaged in life with us. Problem solving in any other arena was for another time. This was a time to experience God and each other.

All the sessions were successful beyond all expectations. But my heart remembers all the moments in between sessions when the facilitators gathered to prepare themselves for the next session. When they joined together in between sessions, the excitement and energy of the day was electrifying.

Almost breathless with the anticipation of sharing what had happened in their group session, they came together, not to examine a process, but to live it! Joy-filled tears, the laughter of being connected, the depth of the presence of God, the growing awareness of what we were doing, the excitement of this new activity of being together—all exploded into our meeting place.

But the depth and the mystery came when we prayed together in preparation for the next session. God was entirely with us. We each experienced that connection with God and each other. We prayed for our gathering and our new denomination and our spirits climbed to new destinations. We prayed because it was necessary to pray. We prayed in love and connection.

Our prayers energized us, centered us, and prepared us for the next session. When my leader/facilitators left for their next session, I prayed for them and waited for their return.

While our facilitators were meeting, the rest of the participants had space and time to walk, to pray, to be quiet, to reach out to God and each other in multiple, wordless connections of Spirit!

We had found a well spring of love that was uncontainable and unforgettable. God's Blessings flowed everywhere, filling us with the reality of Spirit among us. Excitement, love, connection, possibilities surrounded and enfolded us in the unforgettable presence of God. We were all changed!

In our contemporary world of machines and electronics, the mystery of direct connections with God and each other is far more difficult to experience and retain in the reality and isolation of our separateness.

I wonder how much we have gained in our electronically superior world. Is God more real? Is life more fulfilling? Are we more spiritually connected?

The loss of spiritual intimacy seems too high a price to pay.

CHAPTER 11

A Traveling Church

What happens if you take the "church" out of the Church?

Sometimes God seems determined to put us into new places that don't feel very comfortable. Or perhaps that's what God is always doing to burn off our resistance to the *new* entering our lives.

The strategy we generally use in response to God's persistent prodding is to create a door of control and defense to protect our right to do things the way we've always done them. This man made door of opposition is fully controlled by us and we have the only key. We will think about, entertain the notion and speculate about opening that door a crack. But we will maintain our control to the death if we choose to do so.

My *church* on the second floor in our sunlit room and *church* in the basement under the basketball hoops were thriving. We had become very comfortable. The stage was set for another God entrance. The questions had begun to appear.

If *church* can happen in a second floor room and the basement of a church, why not a *church* outside of the church? When God asks the question, "why not?" you can be sure the answer is already in place. OK. Why not? The church doesn't have to be limited to a sanctuary in a building designated as "church".

And so the idea of a *travelling church*, a church outside of the regular church, was born and a few brave souls were willing to take a chance and see what might happen. The fact that this opportunity exactly replicated the life of the early Christian Church was definitely a theological fallback position for trying it out.

We met informally for about a dozen Sunday evenings in people's homes, in a random selection of time. We prayed and talked about God. We snacked on special desserts. It was not a raging success. But for those who participated, it opened the door a small crack to the idea that church might exist both inside and outside the walls of the institution: in fact *church* might exist anywhere and everywhere and certainly wherever people gather to talk about God.

And, more important, it became an opportunity to explore what *church* was really about anyway!

It turned out to be not especially comfortable. The familiarity of worship was missing. So what was it we were experiencing? A pseudo-worship? Perhaps. A re-enactment of the early church? Maybe. An experimental ministry? Probably. A more intimate look at the church outside the formality of formal worship in a sanctuary? Likely!

A new/old way to look at church, ministry and the role of the laity, without the limitations and trappings of the traditional church? Yes! The beginning of a new God plan for my life? Definitely!

It would turn out to be the next unexpected step in my unfolding ministry. God is like a "refining fire" shaping us, molding us, empowering us to do God's work in the world, according to God's purposes and time frame. Rarely does it coincide with ours!

CHAPTER 12

God In Four Persons

On meeting Neil.

In the meantime, like so many others, I'd lived with back pain much of my life due to some structural problems that were with me when I was born. It hadn't kept me from dancing, but after having and carrying around three children, my back began to complain. I did the usual round of helping people to keep me moving. Some of it helped for a little while, but age started to enter the equation and the situation got worse.

When walking became an issue, thanks to God and an intervening suggestion, I went to a local rehabilitation center, talked to a back expert, and I met Neil. Neil was six feet, four inches tall. I am less than five feet tall. I looked up. He looked down and we talked about my back for a few moments.

Then, from on high, Neil looked down and asked me to show him how I walked. I did what he asked and felt a little foolish. But wisdom was on his side and my life was about to change! After my required and observed walk, Neil took me aside and gave me a chair to sit on. He spoke and I listened.

"You see, there are three kinds of people", he began. "There are people who move forward and back. And then there are other people who turn around and around." I wasn't sure where he was going, but it seemed important to listen.

"And then, there are sideways people, people who move from side to side in the world. And you," he paused to make sure I was listening, "you are a sideways person! You are definitely a sideways person."

I listened to what he said. I took it all in. And, suddenly, miraculously his words and my spirit connected! I *was* a sideways person. I moved from side to side to get around restrictions or barriers. I moved from side to side to ensure the goal I was reaching for had multiple opportunities for success.

Certainly, I was God's sideways person as I made my way through the mine fields of resistance in getting into and pursuing ministry. In fact, I *loved* the idea of being a sideways person. Neil had reached into the core of my being and discovered exactly who I was. It was a moment of being fully understood by a man who had known me for less than fifteen minutes.

In order to develop my new personhood, and strengthen my back, Neil gave me a stretchy piece of rubberized material to wrap around my ankles to put resistance into my new sideways walking. When I walked in either side-ways direction, the resistance would increase my strength and endurance. Almost immediately I felt stronger.

But Neil had also given me a new life and a new energy that felt quite miraculous. He had identified who I was, not just in my walking, but in my being. In a few short weeks of walking sideways in short bursts of exercise, I was a new person. My pain had literally disappeared.

My *graduation* exercise was the final contact we had with each other. Neil led me to the area at the rehabilitation center where they had treadmills for people to use. Looking down at my eager face, he said with a solemn voice: "This is it. This is graduation". I looked up and waited for his final instructions.

Taking my hand, he helped me to step up onto the treadmill. "I want you to walk sideways on this treadmill. Don't try to go at your usual speed. You'll fall off—not a good idea". I wasn't sure any of it was a "good idea".

But I trusted Neil with my back and my life and he had *healed* me. I wasn't going to stop trusting his last instructions.

I set the treadmill to the lowest speed possible. The machine moved ever so slowly. And then, I screwed up my courage, turned sideways away from the controls, and started to walk with my newly achieved sideways muscles and skills. Neil stood by his creation, watching and providing words of encouragement. He smiled when I twisted around to increase my speed, all the while walking sideways. We both laughed when we realized that I was actually enjoying walking sideways on a treadmill.

But it was more than an enjoyable exercise. It was the triumph of trust over doubt; strength over weakness; new life and possibilities over pain and despair. It was a new identity that had taken on form and life!

The whole experience was a God experience for me: God is always about the business of new life and wholeness. Discovering our unique identity is what life is all about. Finding the courage to pursue new pathways and trusting the hands that can help us is part of the gift of being human *and* connected to God

Neil made it possible for me to recognize and celebrate who I was, grow my spirit and continue the journey. My "Trinitarian" training in seminary expanded to include my "Fourth Trainer". And I was given the gift of being able to continue my work for God. How amazing can God be!

God is everywhere and anywhere, *even on a treadmill*! There is no place that is closed to God. All it takes is our willingness to open our spirit to the unexpected gifts of God contained in the people around us. You will recognize these gifts because they are always "healing".

(I still walk sideways on treadmills whenever and wherever possible, knowing that God and Neil can both take credit for my healing.)

CHAPTER 13

When God Speaks Mountains Move

On Leaving Home and Discovering a New Life

Comfort is one of those subtle but tell-tale predictors of change in the air. We've settled in, found our niche and life feels pretty good. It's not that God doesn't *want* us to be *comfortable*. It's just that God seems to have a penchant for keeping us moving, while we still can move.

Winds of change are usually awakened when we've grown accustomed to the way things are and would like to keep everything in stasis for at least a little longer. Missions accomplished, goals reached. Why not just enjoy the peace and quiet?

Sometimes, a kind of subtle discontent creeps around the edges of our awareness. But it's easily turned away with the brush of the hand or attributed to any number of possible causes that are quite sensible and realistic. We can always think about it another time.

However, God is also the great activator in life, moving in when we least expect this familiar visitor. God may not be "pushy", granting us the freedom of discovery. But God is definitely persistent.

I *was* comfortable. The challenges of being a woman minister in the nineteen seventies were manageable, not finished. But the winds of change had already begun with the experience of our traveling church within the church. And without my awareness, the door to new life was now wide open.

Enter God and suddenly my inner world began to examine possibilities and *what if's*.

What if you designed an experimental church for an interested group that would meet on the first Friday evening of the month? (A person could be part of a traditional church that met on Sunday mornings *and* also a member of this new church on a Friday evening.)

What if you designed this experimental church to discover new ways of shared ministry for clergy and laity? (Shared ministry would mean more opportunities for people to discover God in their life and in the world.)

What if the people shared in the actual worship experience by participating in conversations about God, Jesus, Life, Death, Love, Spirit? (You would now be talking about a new kind of educational process and understanding of Spiritual life.)

What if the worship service included a meal first to feed hearts, spirits *and* bodies? (You would expand the worship experience by adding a dimension of food and life and the collective opportunity to cook and clean up together!)

What if you met one extra evening in the middle of the month to allow for additional questions and concerns? (You would now have a community that was talking about God twice a month through direct dialogue and participation, discovering God in a much broader context in the world.)

What if you added a communion service to the First Friday night gathering to match food for our bodies with food for our spirit? (You would have engaged the gathered community in the most important ritual of the Christian Church, appropriately adapted for this new community.)

What if you found a way to celebrate our Christian Holidays of Christmas, Good Friday and Easter within this new context while allowing time for traditional celebrations? (You would have found a new way of bringing spiritual celebrations into ordinary life.)

What if you found a name for this spiritual adventure and simply called it: "The New Church: A Caring Community?" (You would now have a description and reference point for dialogue.)

What if you found a place where interested persons could gather to have this first Friday night experience? (You would have no excuses for not trying to bring God out into the open in a new setting!)

All my *what-ifs* brought me to a point of decision. It was time to leave my comfort zone and enter a new door of ministry. The work I came to do at my first church had been accomplished. I could stay at my newly established church home and coast in the ease and comfort of a well-established ministry. Or I could heed the whispers and the what-ifs. God would be in either place. The decision was entirely mine.

A plan for a different kind of church life had been birthed. The door felt broad and filled with light. I prayed and waited. A traditional small church became available where we could start this New Church. But that was too much of a commitment too early. We considered meeting in someone's home but that felt too casual. Others options didn't quite fit.

And then *God spoke and the mountains moved.* We discovered a place that was alive with spirit and energy. It had a professional kitchen with all the necessary equipment and it was also a recording space for the Fine Arts Quartet and filled with music. The local Masonic Temple had become available to rent on the First Friday night of the month. It held two other occupants: a small Jewish community which met on Saturdays and all the local Masons.

We held our first, *First Friday* of our New Church: A Caring Community in May, 1979 in this music and spirit-filled location. Our first shared and cooked together dinner was named "Celestial Chicken".

God was the Host and we were all filled! God leaves no one hungry!

CHAPTER 14

And The Doors Wouldn't Close

On God in action when the time is right!

An experimental church is not for everyone. It's too intimate for some; too loosely structured for others. It offers an immediacy of experience that some would find too exposed. But it has the potential to make God very real in every aspect of the experience.

In our lovely, large, high ceiling room where we held our dinners and worship, there were no pillars to retreat behind, no separate space to withdraw. The openness of the room was an invitation to be filled with whatever we could bring to it.

Essentially, the building was one large, very open room. The east and west sides contained multiple, large windows. The northern side was a small elevated stage. The entry on the south included a small room modestly furnished with tables and chairs. The kitchen was open to the large room. We moved ourselves into the space and let God and Spirit direct us.

All the *"what-ifs"* became opportunities to engage in a more intimate kind of church community where God was not only the Host but also the subject of everything we did. First Fridays became a time to learn, pray, eat, share, be silent, talk, ask questions and participate whenever possible.

We developed our own ritual to begin our worship by shedding whatever we could of the interfering baggage we all carry and preparing ourselves for worship. We cooked, ate, cleaned up and made ready for worship by clearing the tables and moving the chairs into an informal seating arrangement.

I provided the teaching materials about God, Spiritual life, our Christian history and the mystery of our faith. I drew from multiple creative resources of sacred and non-sacred literature. Shared questions and understanding became a community exercise; smaller groups provided creative insights. We sang and laughed a lot. The community wrote about their experiences. We prayed and knew that God was present.

Communion ended our worship with a service I wrote for the community where everyone could participate. Mid-month we held another meeting at our home to carry us to the next First Friday. We were a small, mixed community of Protestants from a variety of local churches, officially designated as an experimental church by my denomination, the United Church of Christ.

And then one day, a few Catholics heard about us and came to visit. We were surprised to find how easily they fit into our community. They were looking for the same thing that drew all of us together: a time to know God and an opportunity to make God Real.

But the real surprise came when people from Jewish backgrounds began to arrive at our door step. Undaunted by our Christian anchors, they participated as they could and they stayed. Suddenly, we had become an interfaith community, without ever taking a deliberate step in that direction. Only God could provide that depth of diversity. We were overjoyed.

Rich in variety, eager to be together, we discovered that our *inclusivity* opened the door to multiple experiences of God. Our religious differences became the wealth of our community and blurred in the face of our common worship. We discovered that God is present *wherever* people gather to learn about God. We learned that simplicity is a powerful tool for knowledge. We honored our grace-filled time with love and celebration.

Most people retained their connection to their church or temple of origin. Both could co-exist and supply different needs. But spiritual connections and open communication became the anchor of the New Church, encompassing all our differences.

Sometimes we operated as a spiritual *half-way house*: a home for people who had been burned out and disenchanted with their experiences in other religious institutions. They'd left their religious roots and disengaged from any connections to former churches or temples. We offered a way back, a kind of revolving door that said, "Come, be with us, rest with us and learn from us. Then you can take this experience back with you to your former community and the word will spread."

Our job was to reflect God's love everywhere, not to hang on but to let go and let God be in charge. It was a gift and a blessing: a community rich in God.

We were together for twenty-five years. Friends came and went; people died; new people arrived. Spiritual lives were shared and celebrated; love and grace given and received. We still meet occasionally for a reunion of love and communion and to remember our small community in all its amazing diversity and strength.

The New Church turned out to be a forecaster of the future in its inclusivity of membership, its interfaith dimension and its willingness to look at ministry as a shared activity between both the ordained ministry and the *called* laity.

But more than that, it was a flow of God in the ordinary world, especially for those who would say they were *spiritual but not religious*. It gave them a new way to be *religious* in an environment that welcomed and cherished their *spirit*.

In our research, we would discover that "spirit and spiritual" are powerful expressions of God experiences. In New Church we learned that religion can be expressed *spiritually* when the focus is on God experiences in each of our lives and in all aspects of living. Our individual differences turned out to be rich opportunities for spiritual growth.

Praise God from whom, *and for whom,* all blessings constantly flow.

CHAPTER 15

A Story About Bethlehem

When God Visited our House One Christmas Morning

It was Christmas Eve and life is always hectic on Christmas Eve. Some presents were still unwrapped; last minute shopping was in that awful stage of recrimination—why didn't we do this sooner? The house needed to be cleaned because New Church was coming in the morning for our Christmas Day service. And we had to go to a family Christmas Eve party.

It would have been better if we could have come up with an excuse for not going to the Christmas Eve family party. But we didn't have the heart to say "no" at the last minute on Christmas Eve. We just wanted it all to work out!

Surprisingly, everything fell into place. The house got clean, gifts were wrapped and we showed up for the Christmas Eve party feeling pretty smug about the whole thing. Christmas was going to happen another year!

Except that God had other ideas of how to make Christmas real besides clean houses and wrapped gifts.

The party was filled with people and children and presents and noise and all the normal activities of a family gathering. But we stayed too long. It was nearly midnight when we left to drive home. Exhaustion caught up with us and Lew and I got into one of those *impossible to understand* arguments about nothing and everything on the way home.

We solved nothing, yielding no power or credibility to the other and falling into bed exhausted for only a few hours of sleep. The New Church was having their Christmas Day service at our home at 8:00 a.m. At 7:30 a.m. we were still unresolved and disconnected. We both felt lost in this impossible situation and the distance between us.

At 7:45 a.m., I suddenly discovered exactly where we were!

"Lew, last night . . . that was Bethlehem! That was what it must have been like when Jesus was born. All the people milling around, families being and doing what families do; crowded with people, food, activities—all the messes of living with multitudes of other people: an ordinary place where an extraordinary event was about to take place!"

It *was* true! We were in our own Bethlehem, in all the stressors and strains of this extraordinary holiday . . . and *God* was about to be born! The New Church people arrived and found us both in tears.

And the Christ Child was born with the entire church in attendance.

It was another profound lesson in knowing God in the middle of life, calling us to drop all extraneous and troublesome issues and focus on those critical moments when new life appears and all of life is changed. God is always a partner in those moments that transform our lives—a powerful mid-wife in every new being. Amen!

CHAPTER 16

Paul's Story

A Special Story about our modern day "Paul"

Paul was a member of the New Church, almost from the beginning. He was also a patient in my practice as a psychologist. We had worked for many years on important issues that had brought him to see me. The New Church provided him with a spiritual environment that deeply enhanced our work in therapy. Paul was a special person, deeply valued by the community for his wisdom and simplicity.

When I moved my practice as a psychologist to a new addition we built on our home, Paul's life entered a new phase of treatment that was unexpected and quite beautiful. Paul was about to be *healed*.

The waiting room to my office was entered through a short flight of stairs in the side yard. Once inside the waiting room, the door to my actual office was to the right; straight ahead was the door to the inside of our home. On Wednesdays, when Paul had his appointment at 12:30, our two year old grandson named Mikey also had an "appointment" to play with Lew inside the house. Paul would arrive a few minutes early. Mikey would be dropped off at precisely 12:30. Paul would sit in a chair in the waiting room. Mikey would have to pass Paul to get inside the house

I had prepared both Paul and Mikey for their encounter. They both accepted the situation with ease. They learned to say hello. Paul would always inquire as to Mikey's state of life to which Mikey would smile and head for his play event. Soon they were carrying on small conversations which, between a 75 year old man and a two year old boy, were both charming and very special. It became our Wednesday ritual, and soon it was as important a part of the healing process as the time he spent in my office.

In an extraordinary way, Mikey was *healing* Paul. His few moments with a normal, well-loved two year old, became a healing balm for the unloved two year old that Paul had once been. As Mikey arrived to play and be loved, Paul could absorb what it meant to him to be loved by all the New Church people and me and to see the fruits of all that love in Mikey and in his life.

All that love was contagious and healing.

But Paul also had emphysema and lung cancer. They both worsened and Paul needed surgery. He recovered from his first surgery but it was costly in terms of his endurance and strength. A second surgery became necessary. His recovery was difficult and slow. We were all concerned about his ability to continue his life. When a third surgery became necessary, Paul knew he could not survive the ordeal.

His spirit was resilient; his mind clear; his family was with him. A nearby Hospice provided a caring environment in his home for the duration of his life. When it was apparent that Paul was running out of time, he asked me to bring our New Church Communion to him, as his last meal before he died.

Paul and Lew and I read our New Church Communion Ritual together. We prayed together as a community of Love. We shared the communion elements in the peace of knowing that Paul's pain was ending. Our New Church community was praying in other places. God was entirely present to all of us.

Life had become complete. Surrounded by love, held in the Presence of God, healed by the reality of his life well lived and loved by so many, it was time to let go. We left our Paul with his daughters for his final moments, at his request.

But his courage and his spirit have never left us. In his open acceptance of his death, he brought both the reality and power of the end of life into a framework of peace. He was finished with life and ready for whatever would be the next step in the *mystery* of life and death.

It was not necessary to *know* the future, only to *enter* it.

God is with us through the entire life journey and into the beyond spaces we cannot see. Relying on Jesus' experience of life, death, and new life/resurrection, we have a powerful, new message of God's Love and Presence transcending this life into an unknown future whenever the time is ready for us to take that journey of trust and love.

Death is the door into the great mystery of life. For each of us, it is the same door.

CHAPTER 17

The Winds Of Change Arrive

God on the move again!

The New Church was now thirteen years old, enjoying a life that was rich in God and people, and the rewards of being almost entirely spiritual in our time together. We continued to be a small, interfaith community of Protestants, Catholics and Reform Jews, and one Orthodox Jew who spent time with us before returning to his tradition.

I wondered if we would ever be able to contact the Muslim Community in Chicago to complete our Abrahamic outreach. It was a hope, a dream and a fervent wish.

The year was 1992. I had thought other communities like the New Church would appear on the scene. Churches were seeing the first signs of economic problems. People were beginning to look for something "more" in their religious life. Change was in the air—you could sense it in the surround sounds of life.

But the resistance to such change was equally apparent. We were all trying to hold on to the familiar and safe. Change becomes an immediate threat to the status quo and questions the permanency and security of our lives at a fundamental level. We don't want life to be different if it's going to cost too much of us.

Once again, I first felt the shift inside. It began with a question and an answer: "If I had such a powerful experience with God that transformed my life, aren't there millions of other people who have had similar experiences with the presence of God in their lives?" And the answer was simple, "Of course!" Time passed as that truth moved into my life and took up residence.

About eight months later, the question returned with more urgency. "Now really, if it's true that millions of other people are having similar God experiences, then don't you want to talk with them?"

The dialogue had begun, and with it the start of a plan. The best way to talk to people about God in their life would be to do a study of Spiritual Life in my denomination, the United Church of Christ.

The unusual diversity in the United Church of Christ would make it an ideal sample for such a study. I could also find ample diversity in the Chicago area with no trouble. Everything looked promising.

I could do the study, continue the New Church and keep my practice as a psychologist going because everything was available right here in Chicago. Green lights were everywhere. I was ready to move ahead but felt I needed denominational approval to do the study. I was certain they would be as excited about the study as I was.

But I was very wrong. When I told the denomination about the study, they were friendly, though remarkably frank in their response. "No one is interested in spiritual life in this denomination. So why would you do that?" Without thinking at all, I spoke the words that both affirmed my plan and reassured the denomination that everything would be just fine.

"It's OK. I'll pay for the study myself!" I cut straight to the core of the moment. Money is always an issue in the church. Apparently, so is spiritual life.

The *unspoken* dialogue probably went something like this:

> Denomination: "That's a really crazy idea. But she's a nice lady and we don't want to tell her she's crazy".

> Me: "I know you're wrong and I can figure out how to pay for a small study in Chicago".
>
> God: "Go for it!"

With great relief to be off the economic hook, the denominational people actually said, "That's fine. But we're still afraid that no one will talk to you about spiritual ideas, so you better invite a lot of churches to participate because most of them will turn you down."

I replied that I appreciated their concern and care but was still sure there were many, many people in Chicago who would talk to me, more convinced than ever that they were wrong. Resistance usually fires up our energy and convictions. I knew God was in this new idea. My life had been so altered, I simply couldn't *not* look for others to share what God had brought into their lives.

It was a message the church needed to hear. But more importantly, it was time for people to understand the reality of this personal God who enters into life where we are living it and offers us the opportunity to be transformed by God's actual presence in each of our lives.

And then, *God* slipped an unexpected thought into the moment. "Maybe they're right in wanting you to extend this study beyond Chicago. Maybe you ought to open this study to a research population that will reflect ALL the diversity in this denomination: economic, geographic, preference, size, staff, training, location. The only way *to prove them wrong* is to make this a legitimate, statistical study of my actions in the world. You can do it!"

And I knew God was right!

In 1994, I met with some friends who knew the denomination and statistical sampling. We looked in the book containing a list of the 6100 (at that time) United Church of Christ churches located all over the United States.

It took two years to find a nearly perfect sample of one hundred churches that would reflect the powerful diversity within the denomination. Meantime, I put together a simple plan that would allow people to share their God experiences by inviting these one hundred churches to let us come to them and ask two questions of anyone who would talk with us:

1. What are the *words* you associate to the words, "Spiritual Healing?" (That term seemed to adequately describe the process.)
2. What *stories* do you tell about "Spiritual Healing" from your own experience or having heard from others.

We assured everyone that we were not "spiritual healers" and we didn't *do* spiritual healing. We were just there to listen and record what people had to tell us. To ensure I got all the information I could, I wrote a nine page questionnaire with qualitative and quantitative questions that I would ask each participant to complete—while I was still there.

In January, 1996, I sent a letter to the pastors of these one hundred churches describing our study and held my breath! Within two weeks, I received ninety-six *Yes's*! Some said "How fast can you get here?" Others said, "How long can you stay?" Four other churches heard about us and requested to participate. Naturally, they continued to add to our diversity and statistical reliability. No surprise!

We now had one hundred churches in our sample, located all over the United States: from Maine to Florida; Seattle to Dallas; to the Rockies, the mid-west and all points in between. In our moments of praising God and feeling overwhelmed with the generosity of this sample, I stopped for a moment, caught my breath and reflected on the reality of our situation.

"Lew, remember! We're paying for this study ourselves and we're definitely *not* wealthy people. This sample is located all over the United States."

"Remember! I still have my practice as a psychologist and the New Church Community."

"Remember! We still have Mikey and a few other grand children and their parents."

"How in the world are we going to do this?"

And the answer came back, with the simplicity that God, and only God, always brings:

"One at a time!"

PART III

I THANK YOU GOD, YOU'RE BREATHTAKING!

God,

You know everything I'm going to say
      before I start the first sentence.
I look behind me and you're there;
      then up ahead and you're there too.
Is there any place I can go to avoid your Spirit?
      To be out of your sight?
If I climb to the sky, you're there!
      If I go underground, you're there!
If I flew on morning's wings to the far western horizon,
      you'll find me in a minute.
You even see me in the dark.
Oh, let me rise in the morning and live always with you.
      I thank you, God—You're Breathtaking!

Excerpts from Psalm 139
From the Message Bible

CHAPTER 18

God In Two Questions

The Beginning of Two years of God, Joy, Laughter,
Tears and Love everywhere!

In April, 1996, our spiritual odyssey began at an African American Church in Chicago. Not knowing quite what to expect, they fixed a feast of food so we could start our mission filled with sustenance for the journey: beautiful to behold! We were blessed and gifted before we even began.

The short version of our experience was that thirty people gathered to hear what we were doing; they shared their words and God experiences; filled out our nine page questionnaire and surrounded us with hugs and love as we left to drive to St. Louis for our second church.

But the gift of that incredible experience was the overwhelming generosity of God and the people. After we prayed and I explained who we were and what we would like them to do, I asked the group to give me their word associations to the words, *spiritual healing*. Lew made a list of those words on an easel so that everyone could see them. Once the first words were tentatively spoken, the gathered group came to life.

As more and more words appeared on Lew's word list, any barriers to our being there ceased to exist. Everyone got into the experience. One word would lead to another, to a third and fourth associated word, and then a new word would appear and the list grew and grew. Some forty words later people slowed down giving us time to look at the wealth of meaning on our list.

Everyone had an understanding of what these words, *spiritual healing*, meant to them. But beyond those initial meanings, people were already talking about the presence of God in their lives. "Spiritual Healing" was an open door to talking about God. Far from not wanting to talk about anything spiritual with us, as the denomination had predicted, everyone at our first church wanted to talk about nothing else. The words *spiritual healing* held immediate meaning for each person there.

What we discovered was the range of meaning which culminated in the word, *God*. God was the lynch pin, the center piece, the anchor out of which all these other words flowed. What we also discovered was how exciting, how connecting, how spirit-filled this simple question became. And *that* was only the beginning.

Our second question brought spirit into absolute reality and filled the room. "What stories do you tell about spiritual healing from your own experience or having heard from others?" There was a small pause—very brief—and then the first story about God arrived, told with simplicity, honesty and tears: A story of God in action in ordinary life, bringing about a healing of spirit, an experience of the presence of God in one person's life, and a time of praise and gratitude.

After that first story, there was no stopping the stories of God in action. Story after story came to life in this place of blessings and filled each of us with their meaning. God was everywhere in each story: small and large moments with God in everyday life experiences. Not mountain tops, but life as we each live it in the ordinary activities of the day.

In that very first church in our study of one hundred churches, we immediately discovered that the words, "spiritual healing" meant an *experience* of the presence or action of God in my life which has transformed my life. And transforming my life means that God has become *"real"* in my life. God is now a living, permanent part of my existence and my being. God is a real experience of New Life in the middle of my life as I am living it.

Given what we were learning about spiritual life, we paused to think about the people in the denomination who *didn't know* this powerful reality at all. They didn't understand that people *could* talk about God; that people *wanted* to express their gratitude and joy about God's presence in their lives. They didn't know that people *needed* to talk about God in their ordinary lives so the word could be shared with others and God could be known by all people.

They didn't realize what a crescendo of Spirit lay waiting for the right words to release it. *They simply didn't know where the people were.* What a terrible loss to the church and the denomination.

Lew faithfully wrote down each God experience shared. (Later, I would transfer the experiences into the computer so we would have a permanent copy.) Then it was time to pray, give thanks to God and to this assembled gathering. The experience had been beyond anything we had hoped for or imagined.

I asked the group to stay and fill out our nine page questionnaire so that information would be available for others to know. Most of them stayed. As the time came to an end, we were able to give each person our direct thanks for their help and share generous hugs and love. Then it was on to St. Louis for our second church.

Our journey had begun and our hearts were filled to capacity. As we drove down the highway, the words we shared with each other were words of Praise and Love for God's Incredible Presence in our lives and prayers of gratitude for what we had just experienced.

But God was much more real than any of the words we could possibly express. We felt God's *reality* in our hearts and spirit which were filled to capacity and over flowing with God's presence.

This journey—this amazing journey had begun. We knew where we were going physically, but no idea where this journey would take our lives and our spirit. To predict was impossible given the multitudes of people we were about to meet.

We couldn't begin to grasp the life changes that were waiting to happen to us or know what people would share with us about their lives with God. We only knew that God had guided this entire project from the first moment of questions to the present moment of unrestrained love and gratitude.

We were on the road *for God,* gifted with the presence *of God.* Our lives were already transformed and made new. And we still had ninety-nine churches to go!

CHAPTER 19

God On Highway 95

On Discovering Wisdom in an Oasis

Balancing God, the New Church, my practice as a psychologist and being with our grandchildren was a challenge! But God was never more in evidence than when we stopped at an Oasis on Highway 95 between Philadelphia and Baltimore, closer to Baltimore than Philadelphia. A wealth of diversity existed in the United Church of Christ in the Baltimore area and we were on our way to meet with all four churches located there.

Our needs were simple: we needed gas for the car; coffee and Mrs. Field's cookies for our survival, and a map to get us to Baltimore! After attending to the first two tasks, I approached the map display where the "map man" was in attendance. He looked pleasant enough, but we were in a bit of a hurry, so I made my request simple and straightforward.

"Could I please have a map of Baltimore?" I smiled and waited.

His response was a bit surprising. "What for?" he asked.

I wasn't quite prepared for that response so I stayed with reality.

"I need a map because we're going to Baltimore!" There was probably a slight edge in my voice. We were in a hurry and due at our first church in the next few hours.

His response was immediate: "What for?"

My edge became visible! ". . . Because we're taking a Spiritual Healing Project to four churches in Baltimore!" (I wanted to add, 'so there', but thought I had gone far enough.)

His next response was entirely unexpected.

"Spiritual Healing happens all the time. And it's happening right now while the three of us are talking."

Then he added, "And I feel better!" his words perfectly matching his demeanor. It stopped me cold in my tracks, making me immediately apologetic for my negative attitude. My mind was so filled with this unexpected God surprise that I'm not sure what happened next. I *think* we got our map. I know we got to our four churches in Baltimore . . . in time.

Our map man had just given us the entire outcome of our study, in advance. Everything we would find in the rest of our journey had been offered to us by this incredible encounter with a map man at the map display at the oasis on Highway 95 between Philadelphia and Baltimore.

We would learn that Spiritual Healing *does* happen all the time. It happens whenever two or three people are gathered to talk about God. And people do feel *better* after that experience.

"Better" is a marvelous word. It doesn't mean that all my problems or my most immediate worries will go away. What it does mean is that when we talk about God with other people, something in us is so touched by the experience that we do feel better.

Feeling better affirms that God is around and when God is around, life changes *because new life becomes possible*. It's that simple.

In a situation that feels unsolvable, we may find an option that we hadn't seen before. In a relationship that feels stressed and tired, we may look for a new way to communicate. In a situation beyond our control, where we feel absolutely helpless, we may learn to trust that something unexpected may interrupt the experience when we ask for God's help.

Feeling better is an experience of hope when we hadn't seen any hope before.

We got to Baltimore and met with our four churches, sharing our experience with the map man with each one of them. Their response was so positive that we have continued to share our story in every church we visit.

The gift of our "map man" was pure God. We had received the promise and outcome of the study at the very beginning. We could have stopped right there. But having statistical evidence of God from our remaining churches would be an essential affirmation of our study and would require the rest of our journey. It was worth any effort it took to bring that evidence into the world.

We were so personally touched by our experience with this unnamed map man that we determined to try to see him the next time we were on Highway 95 to thank him for his amazing insight. Not too many months later, we arrived at the Oasis with thanks in our hearts, anticipating how lovely our conversation would be and how pleased he might be to hear our words of thanks.

Was he there? No! Had he moved to a different location? Was he sick at home? Was he fired? Had he died? No way to know the answers to those questions. We vowed to continue to try to thank him by telling his story everywhere. And we felt quite certain that God was hanging around somewhere when we met him.

So, if you're ever on Highway 95 between Philadelphia and Baltimore, closer to Baltimore than Philadelphia, and need to stop for anything at the Oasis, please consider approaching the "map man" and thanking him for us!

CHAPTER 20

Two Years On The Road With God

God is always constant, but never without surprise!

From April 20th1996 to April 18th 1998 we travelled around the entire United States in between ongoing responsibilities and schedules in Chicago. Looking back, I don't know how we did it.

Vividly remembering the experience, it was surely an affirmation of God's Presence with us. We did not travel alone.

One hundred destinations had to be reached, all travel plans made while ordinary life continued to operate—with as little interruption as possible—on a non-existent budget. It was a challenge that grew in importance and meaning with each church.

We met in small, large or medium sized churches; in suburbs, inner cities, rural areas or metropolitan centers. We saw churches that were thriving and churches that were not going to make it. We met with churches that contained all the diversity in the United Church of Christ: African American; Hispanic; White or mixed White, Philippine and Native American. We met with a gay community in Boston and a growing number of churches that were supportive and open to the LGBT people in their area.

We met with large churches, small churches, single pastor and multi staff; old churches, new church starts, churches with mostly old people and churches with a growing population of children.

Our journey took us from Chicago to rural Alabama; to the Watts district in Los Angeles, to an affluent church in Bucks County, Pennsylvania; to a church in rural Minnesota; to a very old church in New Hampshire to a large, affluent church in Florida, and to a church in the middle of the heroin district in Baltimore.

Back and forth we covered the country and everywhere we went we heard the same story: people defined spiritual healing as an experience of the Presence or Action of God in their life that was transforming. Transforming meant that God had become real in their lives.

Most indicated they had never had a discussion about this experience in their church. They didn't feel the church was a place where they could talk about these experiences for fear of being seen as weird, crazy or too religious. (They were much more comfortable talking about it in a 12 step program if that were a part of their life.)

They didn't always feel comfortable talking about their God experiences with friends or family either. The same prohibitions applied. But they never forgot their experiences and when given the chance to share them with us, the experience (and the accompanying emotions) returned as if the experience were happening in the immediate now.

People described their spiritual healing as a *change of state*. They believed their lives were changed and that they were different as a result of knowing God in their life. Their problems were not necessarily solved, nor did they feel better physically. But they felt *different*. They experienced a state of peace which transcended a situation they might have been struggling with at the time. In fact, the word *peace* was the most frequently used word to describe their experiences with God.

Amazingly, they told us that simply participating in our study was an unexpected healing experience. We understood that because it had become a healing experience for us as well. In two years of talking about God with over two thousand people, our lives were clearly transformed and permanently altered by the experience.

The God experiences people shared ranged from short, intimate interactions with God: "I discovered God in my closet"; to an entire group of men taking a fishing trip in the boundary waters near Canada who discovered God when they were all struck by lightning in a violent storm and lived to tell the story.

We heard stories from drug or alcohol addicts who found God in their healing programs and people who discovered God in nature or in grand parenting experiences. People shared God experiences in every conceivable place and situation.

There were no restrictions or limitations to where God might be encountered, if one were open to discovering God. But rarely did people find God in their church experience. It was a consistent and surprising theme throughout the study.

We began to see a picture of what was happening in the church and the growing gulf between the leadership of the denomination and the people in the church. They each seemed to have different pictures of God's Presence in the world and in the church.

Every place we went, we found a group willing to pray with us, share their words and God experiences and fill out our questionnaire. In every location we visited, people spoke of God with reverence, humility, joy, tears, hugs, laughter and with a wholeness and peace that permeated and transformed the entire meeting. Our commitment to the work we were doing grew stronger and deeper with each encounter.

It *is* good to be able to talk about God. It *is* healing to talk about the abundance of God in the world. It *is* extraordinary to be able to pray together and acknowledge the God gifts we've all been given. There is a wealth in God experiences that could transform the church and life from the *inside* out.

We saw this reality especially in our African American churches where the gift of God was not only visible, it was audible! Preaching, music, dancing all spoke of triumph over tragedy; joy over sorrow; life over death!

But in our Native American Church we found a different picture.

The last church in our one hundred church study was a Native American Church in South Dakota, located on a reservation with no slot machines. It was dirt poor. The pastor had led this small flock for several years. Part of his job had been to heal wounds inflicted on many Native Americans by other religious groups trying to persuade them to give up their sinful ways and their religious affiliations. These *good intentions* had deeply damaged his congregation which still bore the pain of such judgments.

The Pastor interviewed us for a full hour before we could even talk with his people. The stories were set in deeply painful situations. But their one constant was God, and not God's imposters. They spoke quietly to us of the God who had reached out to them. We listened and understood that their healing was beginning, but it was not finished. We were deeply moved by their trust and pained by their situation.

As we visited our one hundred churches, we always asked the pastor of the church to be with us at the meeting. We wanted them to hear what their congregation had to tell them about God. Gratefully, almost all were willing to be with us. However, we also discovered that most of our pastors were not willing to share a God experience that had happened in *their* lives. Occasionally they would share a story they'd heard from a member of their church. But mostly, they listened or left early because they had work to do.

We had a growing awareness that the constant and hard work of ministry was taking up all the time and spirit a pastor had. Survival had become the focus of their church: diminishing resources of money, people, and support had taken over their attention allowing for only a few moments to engage in their own spiritual lives and almost no one available to share those experiences.

Ministry was claiming too much time and energy. Consequently spirit was disappearing in the lives of both pastors and churches. They are interlinked in the practice of ministry. The problem had become endemic in the church.

We realized that the immediacy of response inviting us to come to share our spiritual project (one hundred churches saying *yes* in just two weeks) had revealed a profound truth. Spirit was losing ground everywhere—a deeply painful loss, shared between the pastor and continuing in the congregation. We represented a step, any step toward spiritual renewal and hope.

The loss of spirit was killing the church in subtle and not so subtle ways. And no one seemed to have any ideas or plans for damage control.

One pastor wrote about the situation after our meeting at her church. "On a personal note, I realized that the busyness of my ministry has once again overwhelmed that awareness, that expectancy that I used to have more readily at hand as I awaited those moments of insight and revelation that have been part of my past life's journey.

Logically, I know that ministers need support systems and communal spiritual nurture, but that we tend to fall back behind as the work of ministry takes over once again.

Thank you for the reminder that I can find my way back again to that renewed sense of the presence of God. I long for a continuation of what we lived the other night—just as surely as anyone else there."

Each church had its own story as well as the stories of those who came to talk with us. Two churches stand out in our memory as never to be forgotten pictures of God in action in the world:

1. In 1996, we met with a group at Old South Church in Boston. The church was a large, very active church in downtown Boston. The group that gathered that night were all members of the AIDS support group at the church.

At that time, Aids was a dreaded disease with terrible fears associated with contracting the disease. We knew little about Aids and it was fast becoming the 21st century version of the plague or leprosy. In fact, people were so frightened about the possibility of this disease spreading through simple hand contact that people with Aids had become the "untouchables" of modern time.

Those fears were enacted by refusing to hug a person with Aids and eliminating physical contact except in quarantined situations in hospitals. We didn't know about the disease and only had our fears to guide us.

The church in general didn't know how to deal with the situation any better than anyone else, with the exception of Old South Church in Boston. At that church, the pastor formed the Aids Support/Prayer Group which met regularly to pray, to share their pain with each other and with their pastor who was not afraid to be in contact with each person. Sharing a hug, holding, praying became normalized activities, removing the terrible strictures that had been placed on personal contact.

Our group shared the desperate reality of being ill and not being able to receive the touch of care that might have eased their pain; the desperate losses they felt when friends died from this disease. They told us with tears of relief how it felt when their minister was able to hold their hands when praying or mourning the loss of a special friend.

Simple touch is profoundly healing and *indescribably painful* when withheld.

We heard their pain, shared their joy in finding one place where they were accepted as whole people. We held their hands, hugged their bodies and knew that God was in each moment we shared.

How far we've come in dispelling the fears that were associated with this disease and finding the means and the medicines to alleviate the terrible suffering people have endured. Thank God!

2. We visited the second church in 1998: A small Philippine Church in Chicago which experienced an amazing healing that transformed the entire church. One of the children in the church, an adolescent girl, had been brutally raped by a young man in the neighborhood. While she physically recovered from the experience, her life became overwhelmed with fear and anxiety.

Rape is a travesty that invades our physical personhood and fills our spirit with fear and dread. It is an unforgettable experience, especially when it happens in the life of a young person.

This small church determined to help her heal. They started with continual prayers for her recovery and healing. Day and night, the community prayed for the girl and her entire family. But they enacted those prayers by arranging an escort service for her among the members of the congregation so that she would never be on her own when going to school, during school hours and returning home. Wherever she went outside the safety of home and family, someone from the church was there to protect her.

Their time was unlimited. As long as she needed them, someone would be there for her.

In that environment of prayer and protective action, she began to heal. Each member of the family was also prayed for on a daily basis because rape is a travesty that affects the entire family. When one family member is brutally injured, the whole family is profoundly impacted by the experience.

The family needed a community to pray continually for their recovery.

But the church did not stop there. They prayed for the person who raped her. They continually held him in their prayers for redemption and healing. Amazingly they were able to transcend their own anger in the knowledge that he, too, was a child of God who needed healing.

In fact, when he was released from incarceration, they brought the perpetrator into the church itself to arrange a reconciliation with the girl, her family and the church community. And they were successful in their healing mission.

When they shared this profound experience with us, we could see what it had meant to the entire church. They were deeply touched by being able to bring God into a seemingly impossible situation.

Their prayers were the glue that held them together to accomplish a healing for everyone.

They never stopped praying. They removed their judgments from the situation and literally turned the whole experience over to God. In sharing the experience with us, it became even more validated by our response. We were deeply moved by another community that saw their mission to all people, regardless of who they were or what they had done.

Spirit in both these churches was alive and well, affirming the presence of God everywhere. We experienced their non-judgmental love expressed to people the world feared or hated. We learned how real God is in situations where the lost need to be found, and the unloved need to be held in hearts and arms and prayers.

We saw God in action healing the world through all the people we were meeting. This is how God works in the world. Each of us is a designated God agent bringing the Spirit and Love of God everywhere. Whenever we bring God's healing messages to another person, we are acting on God's behalf for the world.

The world can only be healed through our combined efforts to bring God's Presence and Love into *present* time. It all begins with one person— transmitting one message—to another person and starting right now.

In the electronic language of today, those simple messages need to become "viral" and transform the world.

CHAPTER 21

Three Waitresses, One Artist And A Woman In A Mental Hospital

When God is found in the world,
New Life is everywhere.

We decided that waitresses are surely God's agents in the world. They help us, feed us, provide us with life's necessities, smile when they may not feel like smiling, and are very accommodating to our idiosyncrasies in food choice and ordering. We tend to take them for granted and rarely tip them as much as they are worth. Yet they continue to provide us with what we want, when we want it, in whatever way we choose, without complaint.

In our study, three waitresses touched our spirits and collectively made God much more real in our lives.

I. The first waitress was about sixteen, working in an informal, nondescript breakfast place catering to people in a hurry. She was sweet, pleasant and very sixteen. We liked her and enjoyed her enthusiastic approach to life.

After we began our project we started praying before meals, even in public. It gave us three more chances to praise God and give thanks and that felt wonderful. Once you introduce that behavior, it doesn't matter whether you're in the privacy of your home, or in a public setting. Prayer is prayer and God is God. They belong together.

We'd prayed, finished our breakfast and walked up to the cash register where our young waitress was waiting for our payment. We did the money transaction and were about to leave when she said to us: "Hey you guys . . . you know that thing you did before you ate . . . I mean . . . well I think you prayed."

I nodded yes. And she smiled at us and said, "That was cool . . . very cool." We smiled in response and agreed entirely. It *is* very cool to thank God for food, for life and for waitresses who notice!

We smiled all day, remembering her words and her enthusiasm. And we were quite sure she would mention our cool behavior to a friend later in the day. And the word will grow!

II. We met our next waitress through a story we heard in our study. The narrator of the story was a woman in her late forties whose husband had unexpectedly died the year before. She was devastated by her loss; the suddenness felt overwhelming; and she found herself unable to move beyond the ongoing, never ending grief she felt.

Later unexpected physical symptoms she was experiencing would add to her despair and compel her to seek medical attention. After tests and a physical examination revealed no medical problems, the doctor said to her, in a surprising gesture of non-caring, "Go home, you're just grieving. You're fine. Just go home and grieve". He brushed her off with a gesture that indicated his annoyance and disinterest. Fortunately, she did not go home.

Instead she went to a restaurant she and her husband had frequented before he died. It was noon and the restaurant was crowded. She was shown to a table in the middle of the restaurant and sat down, still engrossed in the experience she'd just had with her doctor. When the waitress came to the table, she was looking off in the distance, tears welling up in her eyes, and not thinking about food at all.

The waitress, looking at her and noticing her tears, put away her order book and said gently, "Are you OK?"

Startled, the woman answered, "Yes ... yes ... no, I'm not OK. My husband died and I just can't stop thinking about him and how much I miss him. I'm not OK at all".

The waitress stopped for a moment and then said unexpectedly, "May I pray for you?"

Surprised by her words, the woman hesitated for a moment and then said, "Yes, that's OK", assuming the waitress meant at church on Sunday, or at a prayer group, or maybe that night when she was finished with work. The words hadn't yet connected.

The waitress, understanding what was happening, said, "No, I mean right here, right now. May I pray for you right now?"

The woman stopped, thought very carefully about this strange and unusual offering of prayer, and looked at the waitress. Whatever she saw in the waitress's face, she responded with a surprising surge of energy, "Yes, that would be good."

The waitress took both her hands and softly spoke the words of a prayer that reached directly into the woman's heart.

She confessed to us that she didn't remember the exact words the waitress spoke in her prayer. But it didn't matter because they were really speaking to her spirit. She felt immediately healed by the experience of prayer, in the middle of a crowded restaurant, from a stranger who also knew God.

Afterward, we thought how often we may feel the need or wish to pray with someone and hesitate to engage in that healing action because there are other people around, or because it might make someone uncomfortable. We miss the opportunity to connect directly to the healing presence of God with someone who needs to experience that presence.

We vowed to change our behavior.

III. Our third waitress appeared in our lives one early morning after a long drive and almost no sleep the night before. We had been travelling in between churches in Pennsylvania, arriving at midnight at a Holiday Inn on the eastern side of Pennsylvania and needing to be back on the road again early the next day, heading west. Because it was so late when we arrived, we had to park at the far end of the parking lot. We fell into bed, exhausted.

We were almost too tired to sleep and tossed through the night. Finally, at 6:00 a.m., I said to Lew, "Let's get up, get our bags and get breakfast. The restaurant shouldn't be too crowded at this hour". He agreed and sure enough, the restaurant wasn't crowded. However, that meant that nobody was in the restaurant—no cook, no waitress and no other customers.

We sat down, impatiently waiting for people to arrive. Soon they did. First, the customers came, finally the waitress and cook. We anticipated being the first to receive service. But we were wrong. The waitress waited on all the other people, finally arriving at our table last. She was ready to take our order; I was frustrated and crabby. Lew was tired. We ate quickly and left.

In order to get to our car, we had to walk down a long corridor, past the front desk, down another long corridor, out the door and to the farthest end of the parking lot. By the time we were at the car, my frustration level was only increased. I just wanted us to get started. We got into the car, Lew started the engine, and we heard a knocking on the door to our van.

There stood the waitress, outside the door, with my purse in her hand. In my haste to get going, I had left it in the restaurant. Stunned and shaken out of my negativity, I opened the door, invited her in, realizing she had to have run to our car to get to us before we left. She handed me the purse with a look of pure helpful love on her face.

Feeling embarrassed by my crabby behavior, and seeing the unexpected caring in her expression, I hurriedly said to Lew "Please give me some money, so I can give her a tip."

She looked at me and said simply, "I don't want your money. *I want you to have what you need*!" She turned around and left.

We drove in silence for many miles while I absorbed what had just happened. Her words echoed in my heart and mind: "*I want you to have what you need*". I couldn't stop hearing them and thinking about the experience.

Suddenly, I said out loud, "Lew! That was God! God running after us to give me what I need. Ignoring my crabby behavior and impatience; running down the corridor past the office, down another corridor and to the far end of the parking lot to give me what I absolutely need: my purse, which carries who I am and all the necessities in my life."

That picture of God as the *Hound of Heaven* chasing after us came into mind immediately. God in a waitress who gave me back my life, who set aside her own needs to respond to my mistake: Not judging my behaviors, but knowing my need: God with us and enabling us to continue on our journey.

IV. We were in the basement of a church, which is where we usually met to do our study. The walls were filled with beautiful photographs. The photographer was in the gathered group and he was blind!

When our meeting was finished, we had a chance to talk with the photographer. He told us an amazing story. "I took these photographs while I could still see", he explained, sensing our questions. "But I was a real son of a gun. I didn't care about anyone. I made a lot of money.

That's all I cared about. But since my disease—I have AIDS—since I became blind, my life has changed entirely. And now all the women in the world are beautiful and all the men are handsome and I thank God every day for my disease. It has *healed* me!"

And we understood perfectly because we had heard the same kind of story from others who had serious or fatal diseases but felt *healed* by God's Presence in their lives, regardless of the outcome of their disease. We learned a distinct difference between "healing" and "curing". Curing is a powerful and wonderful gift. But healing transforms my life in the presence of God, regardless of whether I am cured or not.

V. We could see this woman was hesitating to tell us her story. We had just finished a meeting at a church in the south. The meeting had been very well attended and people were still milling around and talking after the meeting.

She came up to us and said, clearly wanting to talk, "I've never told this story before," she started, "you'll understand when you hear it. Do you have time to listen?" We reassured her that we wanted to listen.

"I was a divorced women living with my two children and everything started to go wrong. Both kids got hooked on drugs and left home. I lost my job, my ex stopped paying us and I gave up. I didn't care about anything anymore.

I became so depressed I was hospitalized in the locked ward of the mental hospital to protect me from killing myself. I didn't care if I lived or died. What did I have to live for anyway . . . no kids, no husband, and no money. Nothing! And so I just lay in my bed in a kind of mindless stupor.

One day a team of doctors came into my room and I heard them saying, 'If we don't reach her soon, we're going to lose her!' And I didn't care. That was fine with me. I didn't want to live anymore anyway.

That same night, in the middle of the night, a light went on in the corridor outside of my room and the door was pushed open. There, in the corridor outlined by the hanging light bulb, was Jesus and he said to me in a voice that was loud and clear. 'Get up!' No mistaking that message. 'Get Up! You've got kids to take care of. You've got a life. You can't just lie here!'

I knew it was Jesus . . . can't tell you why. I knew and I also knew that he was right. What was I doing lying in this death bed, letting everything in my world go. It was crazy and *I—wasn't—crazy.*

The message was delivered. Jesus was gone. But I realized I had a major problem. If I told the doctors that Jesus had visited me and told me to get up, they'd have thought I'd really finally gone crazy and I'd never get out.

I needed to convince them that I had finally hit bottom, was ready to come up, get out and find my kids. And I did! I found them and we moved to Florida. I got a job."

She looked at us to see what we thought of her story. We were so filled with her miracle that all we could do was to hug her, tears all around, and thank her for sharing her experience with us.

We were living a miracle every day: God in action, Jesus in action, Spirit in action. Blessings were everywhere.

All the negative expectations about the outcome of our study from the denominational hierarchy had long since disappeared in the reality of God in the world. The proof of God-Present was mounting with each church. By this time we knew, with no questions or doubts, that God was absolutely real in the world. We also understood that it was critical for the church to know this as well. Their survival depended on it.

We believed that if we were able to disprove their negativity toward spiritual life by proving how real God was for this amazingly collected, randomized population of churches, the whole denomination would be enriched and would grow in Spirit everywhere.

Unexpectedly and sadly, it would turn out that we were very wrong. *This was a message the church couldn't hear.*

CHAPTER 22

The Protestants Are Coming!

Just when we thought we were finished, enter God!

We were feeling pretty smug. We had finished visiting our one hundred churches in the United Church of Christ. We had travelled the country, talking with over two thousand people. Everywhere we went, we were welcomed. Each church provided us with a group of people who wanted to share their God experiences and pray with us. Eighteen hundred people had filled out our questionnaires and we had collected hundreds of stories.

We were in absolute awe of this experience that had claimed two years of our lives and filled us with such profound joy. Even the turmoil and messiness of traveling didn't diminish our spirits. We were re-energized with each church we visited.

As a symbol of our journey, we found a very large map of the United States, hung it in a prominent place and visibly marked every church we visited. Walking by it several times a day was a profound reminder of God and all the people we had met. God was alive and well and so were we. We had actually done it all!

It was a familiar setting for God to re-enter our lives and stir the waters again.

"What about the Catholics?" whispered God one day; "You might find them interested." I hadn't thought about that at all. I thought we were finished.

Almost the next day, one of my patients in my practice casually mentioned a program she was attending that week. "I'm going to hear Jack Shea speak on Friday. You might be interested in hearing him." She and I often talked about spiritual issues. She was an active and devout Catholic, and very open to new ideas in the church. Jack Shea was a Catholic theologian with a renowned reputation for . . . story telling!

I smiled at God's rapid response and we went to the lecture. After it was over, we introduced ourselves to Jack and talked about our project and God's new *suggestion* we might try bringing our study to the Catholic Church. I thought he'd probably be polite but not very encouraging to these two Protestants and their request.

Not only was he interested, he made arrangements for us to see the priest in charge of the Catholic Archdiocese of Chicago and he found a woman who would match our sample, ethnic diversity for socio-economic diversity in the greater Chicago area.

We spent the next year meeting with a dozen Catholic Churches, collecting words and God experiences, completed questionnaires and enthusiastic responses everywhere we went. To our surprise, we discovered we were hearing the same words to describe God and listening to very similar stories to those we heard in our Protestant churches.

It was as if the Catholic Church were a continuation of everything we had heard in the Protestant Churches. With the exception of specific Catholic references to the mass, priests and nuns, you could have mingled the experiences and the questionnaires and come up with one large sample of undifferentiated Christians.

In one church, before we arrived, a telephone call chain announced our presence: "The Protestants Are Coming! The Protestants Are Coming!" We were indeed. Our new life had just begun.

But it wasn't over yet.

As soon as our Catholic study was complete, once again, metaphorical whispers from God entered the scene. "What about the Jews? Why don't you see where they are?"

I tried to bargain a bit with God. We've already done the Protestants and Catholics and that's been absolutely marvelous and we're so grateful. I wouldn't know where to start with the Jews.

Then I stopped and remembered (how could I forget!) that thirty years prior, I had done my doctoral dissertation with women from Protestant, Catholic and Jewish congregations in the Chicago area. Do you suppose the Rabbi I worked with at that time was still around thirty years later?

Indeed, he was around, but within a few weeks of retiring. When I called him on the phone I said, "Rabbi, this is Bobbie McKay, you won't remember me." And he said, "I do. What do you want *this time?*"

We would spend nearly a year in the Reform Jewish tradition in the greater Chicago area and in southern Wisconsin. And not to our surprise any more, we found very similar responses to our Protestant and Catholic Churches and more words, God experiences and a willingness to fill out the revised questionnaire I had written to accommodate a Jewish population.

One story will be forever remembered in our experiences with our Jewish sisters and brothers. We were in a basement, once again, collecting words and experiences of God's Presence in the world. One of the men in the group seemed to be growing more anxious and desperate with each of the shared stories. Finally he interrupted me. He couldn't wait any longer to be heard and in his desperation raised his voice to a level of shouting!

"I have to say something. I work in a Protestant Hospital and almost every day someone says to me: 'And have you accepted Jesus Christ as your personal Lord and Savior?' and I am offended."

And I replied, "And you should be offended! That's entirely inappropriate!"

Stunned, he looked at me and said, "Do you mean we could talk this way? We could really talk this way?"

I said in a gentler voice, "Yes, of course. This is how we should be talking to each other all the time." He looked at me, as if to say, 'could this be true?'

And I repeated my message. "Yes, we can talk this way. We really can. It's OK"

In fact, he never stopped talking through the meeting, after the meeting and into the parking lot where the three of us stood by our car and talked for another hour.

Can we talk this way? Can we really talk together of the many issues we've been afraid to expose? Can we reach out to each other to look at our amazing God roots and discover how similar we really are?

Can we overcome the barriers we've carried for centuries and talk to each other instead of killing each other?

Can we each own our God roots and connections and discover the opportunities we have to be spiritually connected while we retain our individual religious traditions and lives?

We had found the answers to all those questions to be a resounding *yes!*

We began to think again about whether we could ever find an Islamic connection to add our growing family of God. Would they have the same willingness to share in our study? Could we gather this Abrahamic Tradition into one spiritual voice praising God, sharing our words and God experiences, *while keeping our differences intact?*

In our hearts we knew that God was more powerful than all the divisions between us. We waited and prayed for another one of God's interventions, knowing with absolute certainty that one would indeed come when the time was right.

Our prayer simply became:

> Oh God, may it happen soon!
> The need is so great! The time is so clearly now.
> God willing, we will be able to continue until we reach this reality:
> Christians, Jews, Muslims: All Praying and Praising God Together.
> May it happen now.
> Amen!

CHAPTER 23

Why Are You Discriminating
Against The Episcopal Church?

Re-entering history and changing it!

My friend was kidding around when she asked that question. But I got the message. I hadn't thought about doing the study in the Episcopal Church. When I heard her question it felt suspiciously like God re-entering the scene.

OK, why not? Or better yet, why not see what God has in store.

We found an immediate entry to the local Episcopal Bishop and told him about our work. Not surprising, he issued a supporting letter and found ten Episcopal Churches around Chicago and the suburbs that were pleased to have us bring our study to them. We found one surprise almost immediately: more men attended our study in the Episcopal Church than in any other group we visited. We had about a fifty percent male attendance. Our study didn't cover the why's of that issue, but it was worth noting.

New words and experiences filled in more spaces in our study. But in one of our churches, a woman priest opened a special door for us that had been fully silent.

She was the *first* clergy person to share her own experience of the Presence of God in her life. Always before, clergy had refrained from sharing stories about God experiences in *their* lives. It was OK to talk about someone else's experience—just not my own.

Her story was a powerful experience of personal healing. When she finished, she stopped in astonishment! "You know . . . that's the first time I've ever shared that experience with anyone. I can't believe this. I'm a clergy woman and I never told anyone this miracle of God's presence in my life!"

Pausing to let that reality enter into her being, she grew quiet and then, looking around the group, she spoke again, slowly as if to reinforce what she had just discovered. "I've never told this story to anyone before tonight".

To us, she added, "I am so grateful you are doing this study. It is so important . . . for all of us." We understood her words. It was a God gift we had to share.

Having re-entered the world of my own past life as an Episcopalian, my heart was more than a little stirred by this latest God gift. But God had more experiences in store for me to address that issue.

A few years later, I was asked to give a lecture about our study at the same Episcopal Church I had been asked to leave many years prior. Before the day of the lecture, I thought about that experience that had caused me so much pain and grief. And I rediscovered that amazing truth that we so easily forget.

Sometimes a closed door is an essential part of our Spiritual growth. Often the pain that results from that rejection leads us into an unexpected new life. My having been asked to leave my Episcopal Church home allowed me to "discover" my surprising call into ministry and enter a denomination that would accept me into ordination, years before the Episcopal church started to ordain woman. It was likely I'd never have done this study had I not been forced to leave my "spiritual home".

As I entered the Episcopal church I had left so many years ago and walked up the stairs to the very large lecture hall that was filled with people waiting to hear me, my heart was pounding—so many feelings—so many memories—so much anticipation.

I walked to the lectern, put my papers down and looked up at the wall behind me. There, in a full length, life size portrait, in brilliant color, with collar and ceremonial robe, stood the man who had asked me to leave the church and *never* return.

I looked at him, examining in detail his face, his clerical robes and collar, his serious countenance, his presence in that room.

Then I smiled at him and spoke silently from the depth of my heart and spirit: "Thank you! Oh thank you!"

It was complete. A chapter closed with thanks. It was the end of a journey into the past with a new ending.

And God, the Great Healer, the Alpha and the Omega—the past, present and future—filled the room with Presence and Love.

Oh God of closure; God of new life; God of resolution and surprise.

You are so marvelous!

I love you!

CHAPTER 24

God And The Internet

God on the move again!

It was late, around 11:30 p.m., and Lew was "surfing" the net. We always hoped to end our days before midnight, but never quite managed to do it.

This time he made a connection to a group in England called the Alister Hardy Religious Experience Research Centre. They were located at Westminster College, Oxford, UK and they collected stories of spiritual experiences from *all* the world's major religions. God was clearly in action again. We were all doing the same work.

Further correspondence revealed just how connected we were. The Religious Experience Research Centre had been able to extend their study to many different religions. We were following the same path with our interfaith study of Christians and Jews. We were both finding very similar results with our data. There was no question we had to meet.

It was our first trip overseas which added to the sense of wonder and surprise which had become daily companions in our lives. Like an unexpected turn in the road, we were now headed in a new direction with no idea what was waiting for us.

Meeting the Director of the Religious Experience Research Centre was like encountering an old friend. We spoke the same language and equally understood how important the research was for all of us and the world.

Their territory was the entire world; ours was the interfaith world in America. They had been engaged in research since 1969. We had begun our research in 1996. They were supported by a connection to Westminster College and Oxford. We were on our own with an unfolding dream and passion. They were our first link in the process of bringing an inter-spiritual, *international* world into connection.

While at Oxford, we met with several groups, culminating in my presenting a day-long seminar and discussion with members of the Alister Hardy Society at Oxford.

At the end of my presentation to this sophisticated and highly educated group, I expected to hear critiques and questions about our research design, sample, statistical results and so on. I anticipated that their academic rigor might find our passion not very exact. I was encouraged that everyone listened attentively to my words and stories and didn't seem to fall asleep during the presentation.

What I wasn't prepared for was the rush of hands that went up when I was finished and the surprising words that came next: "Can I tell you my experience?" "I had a God experience—I'd like to share it if you're interested." From around the room came a series of stories about God to add to our collection.

We had come to a brand new setting across the ocean and found God waiting. Another precious gift to add to our growing body of interfaith knowledge and experience! Praise and Thanks to God!

CHAPTER 25

God In The Army & Navy

When a friend asks a question, you pay attention!

I. "Have you thought about the army?" he asked. I was talking with a new clergy friend from a church in Cleveland and I knew from those familiar words he used ("have you thought about . . .") that he was talking about our bringing the study to Army Chaplains. History had taught me this kind of question was always our next message from God.

"No," I responded. "I've never thought about army chaplains, but I believe that's the next destination on this amazing journey of ours."

My friend was a retired Army Chaplain, currently pastoring a small church where we had done our research. He immediately got in touch with his friend who just happened to be the Chief Chaplain of the U.S. Army. Two weeks later, we were in Washington, D.C., explaining our research to the Chief Chaplain who just happened to have scheduled an all-day meeting for one hundred Interfaith Army Chaplains at Menninger's in Topeka Kansas. And he just happened to be looking for a speaker to lead the meeting to be held two months later.

He asked if I'd be willing to lead the meeting. And I, of course, said "yes". God's tempo had definitely picked up.

Meeting one hundred Army Chaplains was like walking into a vast sea of spiritual experiences. Military Chaplains have a "Ministry of Presence" which means they minister to anyone at the place of their need, regardless of their religious orientation.

Their ministry takes place anywhere, with anyone, at any time under any conditions. Religious differences blur in the commonality of God. This is ministry at its finest because it knows no boundaries—only God connections and God's Presence and Love. That is sufficient.

Everything we had already learned, particularly our experience at Oxford, prepared us well for this occasion. Religious differences, that turned out to be avenues of connection, were powerful messages to bring to our chaplains.

After we had shared our research and the amazing things we were learning, it was time to see if any of the chaplains were willing to share a God experience with the group. In response, they thrilled us with their generosity. Each chaplain would write a God story for us from their experiences as a chaplain. Then, any who wanted could share an experience with the entire group.

That plan was much more than we could ever have hoped for. It was an afternoon of testimony and gratitude to the God who had accompanied each of them in their ministry to all people, regardless of religious or non-religious affiliations.

Not surprisingly, tears accompanied many of the shared stories. These experiences were so powerful that the heart had to be involved in the telling and the listening. (We have promised ourselves that someday we will put these God experiences into another book to preserve them.)

When the stories were finally finished and prayers shared, it was time to say goodbye to each chaplain personally. All the words had been spoken or written. This was a time for silent connections: heart to heart, spirit to spirit; life to life: one hundred expressions of never to be forgotten ministry and love.

II. Not to be outdone, we heard from Navy Chaplains within a very short time. The word had gotten out quickly. Having shared a day with the Army meant we had to share an equal amount of time with the Navy.

Our next destination was Annapolis, Maryland where we were invited to spend an entire day with a dozen Navy Chaplains from the Navy CREDO program. The program was new to us but the plan was certainly God in action again, bringing us into contact with another group that was bringing God's Presence everywhere.

The Credo program is a group of Navy Chaplains who minister to navy personnel all over the world. Their work includes endless travelling, conditions that vary according to where they are, and an exhaustive schedule. In fact, burnout is a constant problem with the CREDO chaplains. We were asked to help them reconnect to their spiritual center to be able to continue their work.

Our group of twelve chaplains (in contrast to our one hundred army chaplains) meant we could interact with each chaplain more personally and directly. They were open and ready to hear what we had learned. We connected immediately to their stress and exhaustion and they saw in us a respite and a chance to reconnect to God.

Our day was intense, tearful, hopeful, honest, personal and ever in the presence of God. Each experience led to another shared experience. We were constantly affirming their work and the profound nature of their commitment. Seeing God in what they were doing was critical to their healing.

What they needed from us was simply to listen and be with them. They needed to breathe in the Presence of God and our experiences and feel our attention to their needs. In sharing our experiences of God's presence in the lives of so many people, we gave them abundant spiritual food to continue their exhausting work.

In the intimacy of this special experience, their emptiness was filled and we were renewed in our commitment to our work. We had become one body, blessed and gifted by God's Presence.

They carried our prayers and love with them as we carried theirs with us, renewed and blessed by God.

As a symbol of our time together, they gave us two glass mugs, a beautiful blue color with gold rim and the words "United States Navy Chaplain Corp" and the seal etched into the glass. In that gift is the message they carry for all people no matter who or where they are: God is real; God is for all people. We are all brothers and sisters in God's love.

Come: All who are weary and broken hearted, and you will find respite, peace and love. Amen.

CHAPTER 26

God And Our Questionnaires

Three Unexpected Gifts that Changed our Lives!

Our stack of nearly two thousand completed nine page questionnaires with quantitative and qualitative questions sat in our closet reminding us that we had a wealth of information waiting to be revealed. The problem was it would cost us more than forty thousand dollars to data process these questionnaires. We had run up against a brick wall we couldn't climb.

And so we prayed and waited, determined not to examine their contents without having the professional help we needed.

Time went on and no help appeared. The recorded words and stories shared in our meetings provided an immediate level of information. But the questionnaires held the potential to affirm the data statistically. If these data supported our personal experiences, we had a unique range of information to speak of the profound impact of spiritual life in the world.

Finally, when I had almost given up hope, my older son, a research psychologist at the University of Pennsylvania, called me. "Mom, I think I have someone who might data process your questionnaires!" It turned out to be two psychiatrists at Johns Hopkins who were involved in a research study to train "clean" cocaine addicts to do data processing.

Their rational was simple: If you're a cocaine addict and are able to stop using, you need a skill to help maintain your abstinence. These psychiatrists were taking cocaine addicts off the streets of Baltimore, with no jobs or means of support, and giving them a chance to survive in the world without their addiction.

They were also providing the resources to start a new life. For these addicts, their lives were on the line: a make or break situation. This was not a free gift to make them feel good. This was a chance to learn a skill and a pathway toward a new, responsible life.

For most of them, it was their last chance.

It was a different situation for the psychiatrists. Their carefully planned research study needed subjects to learn data processing and research that needed to be processed. They had the subjects but were short on data. Who was going to trust sacred data with cocaine addicts even with psychiatric approval? Nobody so far!

As soon as I heard the message from my son, I knew God was back again. We flew to Baltimore to meet the psychiatrists and the men who would do the data processing. For $4,000 (one tenth of the estimated cost) we could have all our quantitative data entered into a data base. We'd find the money somehow.

Three months later, our data were processed and we had statistical evidence for everything we had heard in our meetings, arranged by religious groupings of Protestants, Catholics, Reform Jews and Episcopalians. The quantitative wealth in our nine page questionnaire had been released, thanks to the amazing miracle of computers and data processing.

We had climbed a mountain of words and shared experiences in each session to find waiting data from our questionnaires on the other side of that mountain to confirm everything we had heard. What was *spoken* by individuals was now matched by what people said in their *written* questionnaires.

We were standing on rock-solid data that held an unmistakable reality:

> People do have experiences of the presence or action of God that are transforming.
>
> Transforming means that God becomes real.
>
> People don't share these experiences for fear of being seen as weird, crazy or too religious.
>
> People don't share these experiences at church or in other places where they might be judged or critiqued.
>
> When people share their God experiences in a safe environment, the experiences return in a flood of remembrances as if they were happening all over again.
>
> When people share their God experiences, they *do* feel better.
>
> When God experiences are shared in a group setting, the group is transformed. God b*ecomes* real in the group.
>
> After a God experience, people tend to be more loving and less angry. They live more in the present and not in the past or future.
>
> People never forget their God experiences.
>
> Sharing their God experiences re-awakens the experience for the teller and offers the one who listens an opportunity to look for God experiences in their own lives.
>
> Sharing God anywhere is an open invitation to others to discover new life for themselves.
>
> Sharing God in an interfaith setting is the one hope we have to make spiritual connections and not destroy each other and the world.

We now had evidence, in a recognized form, of everything people had told us. The study, begun eight years earlier, was nearing completion . . . . well at least for the moment.

By now we were fully convinced that God's other name really is surprise! So we were not *surprised* when a few months later we were given the opportunity to have some of our data partially analyzed at the University of Pennsylvania. We had received a second powerful gift.

Finally, we were able to start making interconnections in the data that gave us a picture of the remarkable similarity of responses between our faith communities. Instead of relying on our memories and written information about these spiritual experiences between different faith traditions, we were now able to establish statistical connections between our groups.

We had been given three gifts from a totally unplanned cast of people.

Two psychiatrists who initiated a study about addictions and data processing; six cocaine addicts who successfully learned data processing; and one analyst looking for statistical inter-connections between faith communities, with God as the inter-locking connection at the center.

When the data were finished, I suggested to the two psychiatrists they were really engaged in a spiritual study. They didn't buy that idea at all. "No", they protested. We're just doing a research study on addiction outcomes."

But I knew better. They were giving these addicts, living in a life and death arena, a chance at a new life. Our data, which they faithfully recorded, were also giving them direct messages about God all around them.

I hoped that some of them were able to make the connection.

They provided all the statistical proof we needed to stand very tall as we pronounce the words that were given to us to speak, *by everyone who has participated in our study.*

Those words could now be carried into the world with enormous confidence!

> God is Real. God is everywhere. God is Now!
> God is for All People. No exceptions.
> Look for God in your life and
> You will find God waiting.

> The Gift of God is ready whenever you are.
> New Life is as close as your next breath.
> Open your eyes and your heart
> And God will respond.

> Praise and Love!
> Blessings and New Life!

> Amen and Amen.

CHAPTER 27

God, The Parish Nurses
And George Gallup, Jr.

Our questionnaires find a new home!

One day I received a call requesting me to lead an all-day seminar on Spiritual Life for Parish Nurses in St. Louis, Missouri. Every request was an opportunity to share God with the world. With our new wealth of analyzed data, "Yes" was always the answer.

As I was finishing the presentation, a woman came up and said, "My name is Giulia and I'm with the Christian Science Church. I'd like to stay in touch". God's familiar presence was unmistakable. "Of course", I said, handing her a card to reach me. I knew there were no accidents where God was concerned.

A few months later, the phone rang. It was Giulia. "George Gallup was just at the Mother Church in Boston", she said excitedly, "I think he'd be interested in what you are doing. Why don't you send him some materials. I'll give you his address."

Empowered by this amazing God and our newly acquired data, I didn't send him any materials. Instead I called him on the phone and actually reached him. Never pausing to allow him to get a word or question into the conversation, I flew through the entire research project, ending with our newly processed questionnaires.

When George did get a word in the conversation, it was to express his interest and delight in my having called him and to invite us to meet him at Princeton with our processed data. By now, these God connectors had become almost commonplace. But this one was different and quite extraordinary. George Gallup, from the Gallup Organization, was going to look at our study personally! Praise God. You have brought us to the Promised Land again!

We arranged to fly to Princeton and spent several hours together, and then stayed for lunch with this world renowned researcher. We saw first-hand the humility, understanding and wisdom of this very special man. He knew God from his active participation in the Episcopal Church and in a long standing prayer group he attended. From that first unforgettable conversation, our friendship continued to grow in subsequent visits and conversations about God and family and life.

He understood why we had done the study and what we had learned in the now nearly ten years of doing research. We were not only graced by his presence, but we were able to spend time with him at his home near Princeton to continue our conversations for several years until we died in 2012.

George was always in demand as a speaker, writer, researcher and brilliant thinker. The gift he shared with us was his deep commitment to God; his love for family and friends and his constant inquiry into world happenings through the Gallup organization's network of news connections.

He loved our research. He especially loved the fact that only the two of us, with no support from any organization, had persisted in our journey to learn about God in such a statistically correct way—something that even the Gallup organization with its hundreds of connecting outlets had not done in the same manner we had chosen.

He would write the Forward to our second book which appears in the "Afterward" section of this book. His presence in our life was a powerful blessing and a totally unexpected God Gift. We will always miss his warmth, his wisdom and his friendship.

Once again, the process of meeting George was entirely God directed, not controlled by anything we were doing. A whole series of events had to be set into motion for our paths to cross. It took a contact from an unknown person to the woman in charge of Parish Nurse Programs to start the process by arranging for me to lead a retreat in St. Louis. It took another woman attending the meeting who was not a Parish Nurse, but a Christian Scientist, who wanted to stay in contact with me. She had to hear George Gallup Jr. speaking on another occasion at the Mother Church in Boston (Christian Scientist) about spiritual life and pass the information on to me.

And. of course, it took my audacious phone call, which by-passed the usual protections famous people have, to reach George directly. (Another *sideways* opportunity!) And all this happened right after our data were successfully processed through a program organized at Johns Hopkins Hospital in Baltimore by two psychiatrists who weren't interested in matters that were remotely spiritual, only theoretical and practical.

The atmosphere was thick with God happenings.

Our data were blessed and affirmed by our amazing friend whose knowledge of research, data and spiritual life were gifts beyond measure. How deeply grateful and humbled we continued to be for everything that was happening to us.

> And so God appears to the mighty and to the small;
> God acts in the lives of the great and the ordinary.
> God is Presence and Mystery,
> God is New Life and Possibilities.
> And always Love.
> Amen.

CHAPTER 28

God And The Librarian

Discovering an old file cabinet in a closet!

Now that the data were processed, it was time to take the results of our questionnaires on the road for others to share. It would also be entirely appropriate to look for a place where our data could be stored. The local United Church of Christ Seminary in Chicago seemed an obvious choice to start.

In fact, because a clergy friend had a good connection to the seminary, we were able to talk directly to the President who agreed not only to our archiving our data at the seminary but to becoming adjunct faculty as well. A double gift!

We soon discovered we loved teaching seminary students almost as much as listening to people's God experiences. These intensive, one week classes (eight hours per day), were wonderful opportunities for sharing God experiences and teaching students what we had learned.

One particular class was so taken by our study and what we were doing they invited the president of the seminary to lunch one day to tell her that not only all students, but *all faculty* should be required to take our class. There are no free lunches!

Meanwhile, the issue of archiving our data was taken over by a librarian at the seminary. She met me one day at the library door—a soft spoken, smallish woman who had a mission on her mind.

She took my hand and said, quietly, "I know just the right place for your data!"

Filled with secrecy and pride in her choice, she continued walking through the main part of the library, past the individualized desks and reading places, not saying a word, but steadily walking with a delightful determination and the sense of an amazing secret about to be revealed. I followed without a word. Her manner was so enticing that I knew God had to be a co-conspirator!

We walked up a short flight of stairs to an open area. She turned around and cheerfully said, "Not here!" We walked past a lovely reading area with bookshelves, files and comfortable chairs and tables. She looked back and smiled, "Not here." If she had been a young girl, she would have giggled with anticipation.

We walked further and up another few stairs, down a corridor until we came to a closed door.

We were in a somewhat dimly lit hallway, not nearly as attractive as the other places we had already passed. My delight was turning into discomfort. Where were we? And what was she thinking about? I was getting more uneasy by the moment.

When she opened the closed door, we entered what seemed to be a medium sized closet with a bare bulb light fixture hanging from the ceiling. The floor was an unattractive tile floor with no rug. The walls were old and needed a decent painting. It looked like a closet that had not been used in many, many years.

The only occupants in the room were a large, old wooden file cabinet and the bare bulb hanging from the ceiling. I didn't know what to say. She turned to me with a smile and a wordless expression that said: we have reached a sacred and holy place. Isn't this wonderful! Lost and disappointed, I felt unable to say a word.

Then God entered and the librarian began to explain why this was the most perfect place in the entire seminary to archive our data.

"This file cabinet belonged to Anton Boisen—it's where he kept all his patient records." It was all she needed to explain. Everything she said was true. She was entirely correct and unbelievably wise in choosing this space for our data.

Anton Boisen was known as the "Father" of the Pastoral Counseling movement when I was in seminary. I had been very attracted to his sensitive writing about mental illness and the need for pastoral work in the church.

He understood mental illness to be a manifestation of a spiritual sickness at a time when few believed him. It made him a highly controversial figure in a field just beginning. He was entirely nonjudgmental in his ministering to people residing in a large mental hospital outside Chicago. Not seeing them as *sick*, he saw people as needing spiritual understanding, not merely medical interventions.

He eventually overcame the opposition raised against him and his treatment ideas. The entire pastoral counseling movement came out of his work and his presence with people. He also happened to be buried at the seminary where we would be archiving our data and becoming adjunct faculty.

Did my librarian have any idea how important Anton Boisen was in my life? There's no way she could have known or had any idea that putting our data into his files—even in a second floor closet with a bare light bulb—was a sacred action that would fill me with profound gratitude.

Somehow she knew that our work was a continuation of the gift that Boisen had offered the world, even when it resisted his wisdom. I felt humbled by the connection she had made between us. It was a gift of such magnitude, so unexpected, that I could scarcely take it all in.

I understood even more deeply why his life and work had so touched mine. We had both struggled with major opposition—each in different environments—but over the same issue of God in the world, present to people struggling to live: God meeting people in every place and under every kind of circumstance and condition, ministering to their needs for spiritual health.

Boisen saw (as we were discovering) the spiritual dimension of life as essential to the healing process. We had both followed God's lead, and not been swayed by public opinion to the contrary. So many connections were suddenly put into place.

I looked around that God filled closet-room. I imagined the files that had filled this old, wooden cabinet. I thought about this man who had lived so much of his life with the mentally ill. His courage was an inspiration and a message that all people are children of God, no matter where they live or who they are or how they are judged by others.

I had learned the same message through the now thousands of people who had shared their lives with me. It was a beautiful and deeply humbling experience.

I thanked the librarian for her gift, took a deep breath of God, and closed the door. Wherever they choose to archive our data, our librarian from God had already given us the essential message.

Another Mystery! Another Gift!

Praise and Thanks to God Who continues to be present to us, through other people in other places . . . even in a closet!

Praise and Thanks to God who remains so near and so available.

Praise and Thanks to God for the Mystery of knowing and the Surprise of new connections.

Praise and Thanks to God for each moment lived in the Presence and Love of God.

How can we ever thank you enough for all these gifts?

How can we ever love you enough for being right here, right now, with us?

Wherever we are, you are already there.

Amen.

CHAPTER 29

Making A New Christian Science Connection

When unexpected paths cross, God is always around.

Our Christian Science connection returned through a new door. This time we were actually able to meet Giulia who had contacted me about George Gallup and the Mother Church.

She was our first Christian Science friend and we were immediately taken with her lovely friendliness and welcoming presence. We talked non-stop about God and our project; she shared her life with the Christian Science Church with equal enthusiasm. Knowing nothing about the church and its founder, Mary Baker Eddy, I was intrigued with everything I was learning.

Guilia was an amazing spokesperson and I saw a picture of Christian Science that was remarkably similar to what we were finding in our study. Mary Baker Eddy had simply discovered this for herself a lot earlier and had created a whole church based on Spiritual Healing and God's Presence in the world.

Through Guilia we met Warren Bolon who was one of the editors of the Christian Science Sentinel, an outstanding magazine which published a marvelous variety of articles about God, spiritual life, spiritual healing, and the world.

Warren was so intrigued with what we were doing, he asked me to write an article about our research for the *Sentinel*, which appeared in July 2004. We met his beautiful wife, Holly who became an instant and wonderful friend, and realized that we now had three special friends who were also Christian Scientists. Three gifts from God that would bless and also change our lives!

Our new friends were filling us with their love and interest in what we were discovering. Most unexpectedly, we were on a very similar path with God leading the way. As in our experiences with the interfaith community, we had never planned to go in this direction. But here we were and the path was beautiful.

A few years later, I would do a very small study on the issue of prayer. The question was: "What happens to the person who prays for another person?" My interest was in the process of prayer as it occurs in the life of the one who prays. My sample was quite small: two churches: one a very large, successful suburban church with a prayer group; the other a small Christian Science Church in which the whole church was a "prayer group".

I raised the question first in the large church. Their answer was immediate and unanimous. "Nothing happens to us as prayers. We're only interested in what happens to the person being prayed for. Do they get better or not? That's the only question." The issue was addressed and closed.

The response in the Christian Science church was entirely different. "What happens to us is very special. When we pray for someone who *wants* our prayers, (a key ingredient), we are *always* affirming the existence of God with our prayers. What happens to the person being prayed for is up to God. What happens to us is the gift of knowing God is here with us."

It was a stunning difference.

In the large church, the most important issue was control: Did the person get better or not?

In the Christian Science Community, God was the most important issue.

The gifts I have received from my new Christian Science friends have changed my prayer life. When I pray now for others I am aware that I am both enlisting God's help and reminding myself of the constancy and love of God in everyone's life, mine included.

Our Christian Science connection is like an open door. I marvel at their focus on God's healing presence. Their beauty is in the love that guides all their actions. They know that God is everywhere and in everyone. When you experience their presence, you know that God is also with you.

Our lives were being enriched every day by the people we were meeting and the enormous variety we were discovering in the "people of God". I knew our Christian Science connection would continue. There was so much God in it. How grateful we were for all the people and now all the years of our study that had enriched our lives beyond measure.

We were also fully aware that *only* God could have planned this journey of ours. Filled with surprises—entirely connected by Spirit and Love—God, *the great travel director*, had led us through doors that we didn't even know existed into a world filled with people we didn't know, who would tell us about their lives with God.

Our journey had led us into a brand new world we had never known or imagined before; a world in which love prevailed; new life emerged, and people everywhere were being transformed by the presence of the Living God.

To live within these experiences was a daily miracle beyond all words.

Amen.

CHAPTER 30

On God And Harvard

*A middle west connection brings us
an unexpected opportunity.*

Once again the telephone became a God carrier. "My name is Dr. Susan Sered. I teach at Harvard. A friend from the middle west called me about your work and said I needed to get in touch with you." I expressed my delight in her friend's good advice and waited for more information.

"I'm writing a book with Linda Barnes from Boston University about religion and healing in America. The book is getting ready for publication but I'm told I need to look at your work to see if it should be included." I caught my breath and said something about being pleased to be considered for the book.

She interrupted my pleasure. "Send me some information about your study as fast as you can." I promised I would.

The result of that phone call was the opportunity to submit our research for inclusion in their new book which was already promised to Oxford University Press. Susan suggested we might want to come to Harvard to meet her and Linda and share some of our study with others at Harvard after publication of the book.

Quickly I put together an article and sent it on to Susan. I knew they were within days of shutting the door on any more chapters for the book. Gratefully, they both decided they wanted our story. But time was essential and this was a new kind of challenge to describe our research in an academically acceptable style for this publication.

Susan was our expert editor willing to guide us through the process. We knew this opportunity was a God gift that we may not have been prepared for, but which had to be put into place. Novices would have to become experts.

Professionally, both women were at the top of their fields. Susan was the research director of the Religion and Healing Initiative at Harvard University's Center for the Study of World Religions. Linda directed the Boston Healing Landscape Project, an institute for the study of religions, medicines and healing at Boston University's School of Medicine.

We managed to write the chapter in time for publication with Susan's help in making sure the chapter was academically correct.

Our study became Chapter 2 in "Religion and Healing in America, Oxford University Press, 2005.

The next step was to visit Susan at Harvard. We didn't question that God had been in the entire experience. But what happened next was a total surprise.

When we got to Harvard, we found that Susan's initiative was unexpectedly shutting down and she was leaving Harvard for another job. Linda was very busy with her project. The book would be published the following January, but for the immediate present, neither was available for conversation.

With unexpected time on our hands, and remembering that the Mother Church of Christian Science was also located in Boston, we called our editor friend, Warren Bolon, to see if he had time to meet. He did.

We had the pleasure of spending time with him and Holly and seeing more of the Christian Science campus in the heart of downtown Boston. In sharing that we had archived our data at Chicago Theological Seminary and were now teaching a class there, Warren asked if I would write a second article for the Christian Science Sentinel and let him know how the class went.

The article was published in September, 2004 after our first class in the Christian Science Sentinel. It was titled, "The Spiritual Healing Project Goes to School".* We were archived and published and once again blessed and gifted.

There seemed to be no end in sight to God's interventions in our lives.

---

* Excerpts from the article appear in the Afterword section of this book.

CHAPTER 31

God At A Baseball Game

Discovering a Muslim World in Rochester, New York

In 2008, we decided to move to Rochester, New York. We had three grandsons in Rochester; I had some church connections there. We'd be six hundred miles closer to our granddaughters in Philadelphia. It seemed like a good idea, though in our mid-seventies, it was a bit of a challenge.

It just so happened, as we discovered, there also was an active Muslim community in Rochester. A fact noted, but set aside in the work of moving.

Life normalized after the move and unfolded pretty much as predicted. We were actively involved in our grandsons' sporting activities which were an important part of their lives. With three of them we could be watching an endless variety of sports on any given day.

So, there was nothing unusual on the day that God came around to visit again. It was just an ordinary day at the baseball diamond with an enthusiastic crowd of parents and grandparents.

The sun was shining, the crowd was enthusiastic, and we weren't thinking about God at all.

Except that this particular game was incredibly slow: the innings were long on time and short on hits! And so I fell into conversation with one of the other women there. We went through the usual information gathering time. She was a writer with two children. I was a grandmother with seven grandchildren. She had previously been employed by one of the many businesses that closed down in Rochester during their economic downturn. Now she was trying her hand at writing.

When she asked about my life and I told her about the study, she was appropriately astonished—not an uncommon response when people realize the extent of our research and our passion about it.

Without thinking about it at all, I mentioned my wish to include the voice of Islam in our study. It was certainly incomplete without it. I didn't expect any kind of response other than an agreement that it would be nice to find a Muslim community interested in participating.

To my surprise, her face lit up, she smiled and said: "I'm Jewish—but I think I can help you. I've just been in a documentary film about Muslims, done by a woman film maker right here in Rochester. If you like, I'll try to arrange a meeting with her."

No longer surprised by anything that God was about, I felt that immediate and, by now, very familiar rush of gratitude. I smiled to think about God appearing at a 7th grade, little league baseball game. Why not? We were always being surprised by God's appearances in our lives.

"That would be wonderful," I said quickly handing her a card with my number. The game finally ended and we left feeling that anticipation that something was stirring in our world. The very next day, I received a phone call from the Muslim film maker who would be very happy to meet us. Her name was Mara Ahmed and this was her first documentary film.

Later that week, we met at the local Barnes & Noble. Never having talked with anyone from the Islamic Community—let alone a filmmaker—we didn't know what to expect from our meeting.

Mara was young, quite beautiful, dressed in a very contemporary outfit. She was as interested in us as we were interested in her.

The next part of our spiritual journey had begun. Once again, the pieces had fallen into place: an unexpected inner conviction we needed to pick up our lives and move to Rochester to be near our grandchildren there. A baseball game and a *chance* meeting with one of the other parents at the game; a long game that didn't demand constant attention; a conversation about our lives in between innings; the astonishing information from a Jewish woman about her Muslim connection!

God available when the moment is right! And the moment was perfect.

Mara shared her changing journey to become a film maker. Her first film was an attempt to introduce the American world to the lives of ordinary Muslims living in Rochester, New York. The title of the film was "Muslims I Know". These were American Muslims, not radical Islamists. They worked hard, married, had children, went to the Mosque, had dreams of the future, took care of their children and were thoroughly American in outlook and attitude.

Mara's dream was to enable the American culture to recognize the American Muslim culture as having the same hopes, aspirations and dreams for their families, while maintaining their religious lives as members of a Muslim Community in America. Our connection as Americans was a base line of opportunity that could be enhanced by the richness of our religious differences.

We were privileged to see her film. In spite of her lack of experience, Mara's first film was a beautiful introduction to a Muslim world that was compatible with and actively engaged in the American culture of Rochester. These were the neighbors next door; the parents at the school PTA meeting; the friends who helped you in an emergency; the people who shared your same worries about the future.

In presenting her film about the American Muslim world, she offered the American public a picture of a world they knew little about, but which contained unexpected gifts and connections. This was a film to build relationships and discover common lives and concerns in an environment of the family.

But God was not finished. Mara also served as a connecting person to introduce us to the Imam of the local Muslim Community, Dr. Shafiq, who agreed to meet with us. His generosity of time and understanding, his friendly attention were multiple gifts to be savored. Through his efforts, we were privileged to engage in our first dialogue with the Muslim world.

It was Ramadan, and we were asked to be a part of the "Breaking of the Fast": Lew with the men and I with the women. I dressed appropriately for the occasion, covering my arms and legs and wearing a scarf over my hair. At first, the women were hesitant to talk to me. But when their daughters heard I was a psychologist, they were immediately curious to see first-hand what a psychologist was like. After their daughters broke the ice, their mothers soon joined them and we began our first conversation about God.

I was deeply touched by how real God was in their lives. Not only do they pray five times a day, they also believe that God resides *next to their carotid artery* enabling them to be aware of God's Presence throughout the day and night. To my Protestant ears, that felt powerful and deeply meaningful, unexpected and beautiful.

I felt the impoverishment of our western culture that slips God into life occasionally, but doesn't have the knowledge of God present at all times. I saw the certainty of these women as a way of life that brought God into the center of every breath and every moment: a grounding that was permanent.

After Ramadan, we were able to meet with a mixed group of women and men, friends of Mara's, to start a dialogue about spiritual life in the Muslim community. As we gathered there were a few moments of quiet. This was a very new experience for everyone and none of us knew what, if anything, would happen.

I quietly began to tell them the story of our research, the numbers of people involved, and our dream of finding a connecting link with the Islamic Community. The story has a mesmerizing effect because it is all about God and people rarely talk about God in a social setting.

When the first God experience from one of the people in attendance was shared, we discovered the amazing mutuality of our spiritual lives. The vision and possibilities that surround that knowledge flowed through the room and came to life.

After that meeting, a recurring thought kept appearing. Could we arrange a meeting with four people from each of the Abrahamic traditions to talk about God? Could Muslims, Catholics, Protestants and Reform Jews gather to share their God experiences? Such a simple idea with such extraordinary possibilities!

Another series of *what-if's* began immediately.

What if I structured the meeting so that it was not a religious experience, but a time to share God experiences? *What if* I insisted this was not a time to talk about our theological differences but an opportunity to discover the similarity of our God experiences? *What if* the meeting were designed to be entirely non-political, concentrating instead on the common God we share?

What if we could share our prayer lives with each other in some simple way? Could we actually pray together?

Dr. Shafiq was also the Executive Director of the Hickey Center for Interfaith Studies and Dialogue at Nazareth College. I spoke to him about the possibility of having this meeting at the college where his Islamic Center was located. Meeting at the Mosque would have been complicated by needing to hold separate meetings for women and men. He agreed to the plan immediately.

Now we had to find participants from each faith community who were willing to meet and abide by our rules. I was prepared to intervene if people couldn't resist making comparisons or attempts at politicizing the meeting. It felt like taking a huge step in a great unknown. Could we actually find the people? Would they agree to the rules? Would anyone share a God experience? Would anything come from such a gathering?

On November 8th, 2010, we had our first interfaith meeting at Nazareth College in Rochester, New York. Four people from each religious group arrived *early* for the 6:00 meeting. (A hopeful sign!) Dr. Shafiq helped us set up tables and chairs.

In a breathtaking evening of prayer and God stories, Jews, Christians and Muslims met to talk about God. No one even thought about breaking my spoken rules. The evening was so filled with stories shared, listened to, and reflected on that at 9:00 p.m. we were still meeting as the campus police arrived to close the building.

The evening had revealed that our God experiences were remarkably similar. God was the center of the entire evening and each of us actively revolved around that center. The circumstances among us were different, but the theme was always the same: God is real; God is with each of us; we have a common spiritual heritage; we can continue to talk and learn from each other. God willing, we might be able to live in peace with each other.

It was an entirely unexpected experience that radiated beyond any and all expectations. We had begun our interfaith journey with sixteen new friends, grounded and linked within the presence and love of God. Everything we needed to know was contained in our common experiences of God Present and Active in each of our lives.

The experience was so beautiful, so unforgettable, we carried it with us wherever we went. We knew that God had brought us to a new place with a message that had to be shared. In a world torn apart with religious differences and potentially very dangerous consequences, we had found a God center which could unite us in love and peace.

The promise it contained was essential to the future for all of us. We would surely need many others to help us pursue this *unexpected* path that God brought into our lives. We could not do this alone.

Our prayers were critical to our journey:

Please help us, God.
We would be your faithful servants and follow you everywhere
you lead us.
But the world is filled with people who do not know you;
Who do not trust your loving messages;
And who are angry, afraid and alone.

As you give us the courage to meet this new challenge,
Please fill people everywhere with your presence and your
love.
You are the only voice that can bring Peace into this dangerous
world.

As you have spoken to us, please speak to all who can help us.
Bring this divergent world into your peace.

We pray in the name of Love given and Love received,

Amen.

CHAPTER 32

God In Four Books

Bringing God into the world.

Over the life and years of our study, we'd already written three books as an attempt to describe this amazing gift we'd been given. For people who have not been able to participate in our study, it was an opportunity to let them in on the reality of God's presence in the world and in our study.

For us, it represented a gift of thanks to God for transforming our lives. Each book described a different time in the life of the study. This fourth book is the final connecting link in our journey with God.

Our first book, "Healing the Spirit: Stories of Transformation" was written in the midst of our data gathering. It described how we had begun the study and followed our journey through our Catholic Congregations. We had not quite finished meeting with our Jewish and Episcopal Congregations but were personally so excited about what we were discovering that we couldn't wait to finish before writing a book about the study.

Our new friend, Jack Shea, who had helped us find Catholic churches for the study, agreed to write the forward for the book. Words and God experiences filled the pages from the people who had participated in the study. It really was *their* book and *their* God gifts to others, set in the context of our very exciting journey.

Our second book, "Taking a Chance on God: Exploring God's Presence in our Lives", was written after our data were retrieved and processed from the questionnaires. The book was begun shortly after we met George Gallup. It was his insistence that prompted us to move ahead with the book.

He was so taken with our research that, to our great delight, he agreed to write the forward for this new book. In fact, the first copy of his forward was hand written and sent to us as a special gift. It includes both his original text and all the changes he made. The words needing changing were crossed off and replaced with new ones. That simple gesture of hand writing his forward was a lovely gift that brought the reality of our close personal relationship into a visible symbol. We were very touched. (A *typed* copy of his forward is included in Part V.)

I wrote the third book, "When God Becomes Real: Stories of Presence—Models of Church", after we archived our data at Chicago Theological Seminary. It was an opportunity to connect my experiences as a pastor with what we were finding in the study and its implications for the future of ministry and the church.

This newest book, "Dancing with God: A Spiritual Autobiography" is the fourth and last book in the series. It is entirely about God.

Translating *experience* into *words* is never finished. Each revision is an attempt to make God more *real*. One relies on approximations, similes and comparisons: "God is like" statements that speak to us of that which is beyond our descriptive powers of language.

Ultimately, God must become *real* for each individual person through the doors of experience, conversation, prayer, meditation, thought, silence, other people and simply life lived with God.

Each of these four books is an attempt to help people recognize a God experience when it happens in their lives and to share the amazing journey we've been privileged to experience.

I pray that something in these books will create a moment when God becomes *real* for you and that you will take that God-Reality into the world to share with others. Sharing our God experiences is essential to the process of discovery. If we choose to hold these profound experiences in our heart, safe and protected, then God remains in the shadows still waiting to be known and experienced.

Remember! God is always *surprise* so keep your heart open to recognize new life whenever it arrives at your door step. There is no experience so small that it cannot be included in your lectionary of God experiences to be remembered, savored and shared.

This is the way that God is made known in the world: through each of us recognizing God in our lives and sharing that life-saving experience with others. We join our voices with all those who have come before us to recognize and praise the Living God of all time and place: an unbroken chain of voices and actions bringing God into Life and Light for all people.

Included in all of our prayers is the hope that all the people who hear about or read about our research will open their hearts to the God who resides within them and see the amazing actions of this loving God in their lives. When these actions are shared with other people, the opportunity for God to be truly known in the world becomes possible everywhere!

Each of you has multiple God experiences to share. Let this day be the first of many opportunities for you to talk about God with someone who will listen. That simple gesture, repeated hundreds and thousands of times, will change the course of this world.

Amen and Amen.

CHAPTER 33

God In A Secretary's Mistake

God in a Four Part "Surprise!"

Part I. Guilt is always a good motivator. We had been visiting Florida for several years as a vacation opportunity to leave the cold and snow of the mid-west behind us. It also turned out to be a special opportunity to re-visit my religious roots by attending a small Episcopal church in Vero Beach.

However, each year I felt a growing sense of guilt about not attending services at a church in my official denomination. Ultimately guilt won and I made an appointment with the secretary of a large United Church of Christ Church to meet one of the several pastors there and introduce myself. My guilt could be released!

Our study became the focus of my visit. It is so compelling, so full of energy and spirit that anything else I might talk about seemed superficial or unimportant. My new clergy friend agreed entirely. In fact, he became so excited about our work that he talked about the possibility of my leading a three day retreat for Florida clergy and laity in a few months. As far as he was concerned, it was a "done deal". I had certainly come to the right person.

God in action again! I was prayerfully grateful for the results of my guilt.

At the end of our conversation, after excited thanks and plans had been put in place, he leaned forward, and in a much softer voice he asked a very strange question: "How did you get this appointment with me?"

Realizing he wasn't joking, I answered honestly: "I called your secretary and she made the appointment".

He leaned back in his chair, thought for a moment and said: "She has strict orders not to make an appointment with anyone I don't know without checking with me first!" He was quite serious. She hadn't checked.

A moment of silence followed. I didn't say a word, and then we both understood. God had already entered the scene and was busy creating an entire future agenda. A secretary had made a *mistake* that would turn out to be exactly the opportunity we were looking for to take our data and turn them into a program that could be used by anyone, anywhere. The timing was perfect!

Part II. A few months later, I led the three day retreat for clergy and laity in Florida. It was 2008 and people were already aware of the decline in church attendance and the growing loss of financial support for many churches. People and their money were leaving in droves. A crisis was growing in many denominations which could seriously diminish the work the church could do.

Our study and its powerful implications became the agenda of the retreat. It was the right time and the right place for Spirit to surround us with possibilities and new life. Everything that had come before in our research could instantly be put to use in actual church setting. God was definitely on the move!

Attending the conference was Dr. Fred Fourie, pastor of Cocoa Beach Community Church, who remembers my saying to him, "We have work to do together". He responded by inviting me to come to their Church and bring Spirit with me. It was an offer I could never have refused.

Once again, God's Timing was exquisite. Our data gathering was complete, processed and examined to find the wealth of spiritual information it contained. All we needed was to convert these data into a program churches could use to open people's hearts and minds to the reality of God's Spirit in the world.

Our data could come to life in a local church willing to try a new program about God. And we could find out if the program actually worked. God the great organizer at work again! All I had to do was to write the program!

Part III: All the pieces came together. The data were easily set into a program called "Making God Real in Religious Settings: Building Spiritual Life Teams". (Later the program would be expanded to include Spiritual Life Teams in Non-Religious settings.) These teams would become a universal opportunity for sharing spiritual life, anywhere, anytime with anyone.

Spiritual Life Teams became the vehicle for people to explore and share their meanings for the word, "spiritual" and their God experiences in a small group setting. It became an opportunity to learn to pray out loud and to share their God experiences with others in the congregation and the community. The entire agenda was to make God *real* in multiple lives and locations. For many it was the first time they had ever engaged in specific spiritual activities that included talking about God in my life and praying out loud together.

My writing a workbook and leader's guide for the process would enable churches anywhere to build "Spiritual Life Teams" and the program could multiply. (More information about these programs is available in Part V of this book.)

From the first team at Cocoa Beach came four more teams at Cocoa Beach. A small church in Miami asked if the whole church could become a Spiritual life team. They suspended all church meetings for thirty days while they concentrated on enacting the program in their community.

Teams began in several other locations in Florida carrying exciting new opportunities to bring God more directly into the life of the congregation. Multiple teams in a church setting offered amazing opportunities to build spiritual life within the congregation as well as in the community.

God was becoming very alive and *real* in several congregations, including one team which combined two different *denominations* with one shared Spiritual Life Team.

When we returned to Illinois, a church that had generally not done much in the way of spiritual life opened their hearts and doors to five spiritual life teams. The program, in its agenda and simplicity, worked everywhere it went.

Part IV. God continued to whisper into my heart. You could try an interfaith program here in Florida. It would be persuasive evidence if you got the same results you did in Rochester. I heard and understood. But it felt a little chancy. What if people in the south weren't interested in an interfaith program? We'd have to find the same population of four people from each tradition to make any kind of comparison. I knew how to get four Protestants from Cocoa Beach Church but that left twelve others missing.

The agenda would be the same: No politics, no persuasions, no religious talk, only prayers and God experiences. Could we find people willing to abide by the same rules? Enter God and all our problems were solved.

We discovered the owner of the fitness center we used was a Catholic. He was young, energetic, successful and very personable. We invited him to dinner and pitched our cause. Would he be willing to be a part of our program *and* find three other Catholics to come with him. He said an enthusiastic "Yes".

We found a woman Cantor at a Temple in the next community who was studying to become a Rabbi. After a high energy, very spiritual conversation she was more than ready to join us and look for three more people from her Reform Jewish Temple.

Our Muslim contact was still missing. From a series of conversations, we discovered a clergy woman teaching World Religions in the local junior college. We invited her over for coffee and shared our story and our dreams for an interfaith meeting. She just happened to know a young student in one of her classes who was a Muslim, a surfing expert and the secretary of the Mosque.

We spoke with him about our dream and he assured us he was interested and could find three other Muslims. Everyone felt certain they could find the rest of the people we needed. We were overjoyed.

On Sunday evening, April 22nd, 2012, we had our first interfaith meeting at Cocoa Beach Community Church in their large community room. Four tables and sixteen chairs, replete with chocolate chip cookies and refreshments, were arranged so we could see each other and learn from each other. We waited, held our breath and prayed!

As before, people arrived early. Our young Muslim friend brought his mother, father and his uncle. We had an entire Muslim family to bless our meeting. Our Catholic fitness center owner brought three other people who had been instrumental in helping him discover his spiritual life.

We had four people and a waiting list of Protestants from our Cocoa Beach Church family. Our Cantor, now become Rabbi, was only able to find two others to come with her. But one was a vocal and wonderful man who regaled us with a story of the trip the Temple took with a local Protestant Church to visit Bethlehem the Christmas before.

With laughter and tears, he described the wonder and blessing of sharing Christmas Eve in Bethlehem with a Jewish and Christian community singing Christmas Carols together while the Rabbi played the organ. Our laughter, mixed with tears, echoed his in gratitude for what we were learning.

For two hours we collected words about God and spiritual life; ate chocolate chip cookies and shared spiritual experiences from each of our lives. Each new God experience brought tears and connections, quiet joy and marvelous laughter.

At 9:00 p.m. our Muslim Family needed to spend time in private payer. I showed them a Sunday school room where they could be separate and comfortable while we waited for their return in silence and prayer.

In our final moments, we simply absorbed the God-filled experiences and prayers we had shared.

We looked around the room to collect a picture of the people involved in this amazing event.

We had shared a time that no one in that room had ever experienced before.

We had become an interfaith community: An Interfaith Spiritual Life Team.

Later that year, we held our second meeting at Temple Israel where our Cantor is now officially installed as Rabbi and Cantor. At that meeting, we allowed visitors to come to listen to our experience as an interfaith community and ask questions. A small group of people came to hear our story and used the time to also reflect on how important it was that we were doing this.

Some expressed deep concern for the Islamic community in the area and the possible retributions that could occur as a result of the worsening situation in the Middle East. It was a profound time of God present, love expressed and gratitude.

In March, 2013, we met at the Cocoa Beach Library where we opened our conversation to anyone in the community who wanted to be there. Our group shared what it has been like to be a member of an interfaith group that prayed together and shared God experiences.

I knew how effective the experience had been from other meetings we had held. In this our first public forum, people sat quietly at first absorbing the gift we had brought. Then their questions and comments affirmed the incorporation of this new experience into their lives as well.

As I listened to our interfaith team publicly talking about the impact of this experience on their own lives, I learned how important the experience had been to them as well. We felt like a marvelously open family sharing a priceless gift with any who would listen.

A fourth meeting was held in April, 2013, at Cocoa Beach Community Church, opened once again to anyone who wanted to attend. It happened to be timed with some of the most troubling situations in the Middle East. Once again, people expressed deep concern for our Muslim family and the community of Muslims in the area, whose lives were threatened by the latest round of hate and anger. We were bound and connected by our mutual love and respect.

Once again, I was reminded of the life-long reality of the interfaith world in my life. From my first group of five interfaith women who wanted to talk about God; to my interfaith study of "Women who Achieve" for my doctoral dissertation; to the interfaith portion of our research study and finally to our growing sense of an inter-spiritual world in which *all religions* might discover opportunities to share their spiritual lives. It was a growing awareness of how important the miracle of these unexpected connections has become in my life.

We have so much in common. We share an inner spirit that reaches out in loving actions to people of all traditions when we allow ourselves to discover our mutuality of Spirit. Beyond our Abrahamic tradition are millions from other traditions who could be engaged in spiritual dialogue with us as well.

Our interfaith work has brought us through a critically important process of discovery to two profound conclusions:

1. Our *shared* spiritual connections are deeply enhanced by the *uniqueness* of each of our traditions.
2. Our *differences* can powerfully support our *commonalities.*

The breath-taking quality of this high risk adventure we had begun was overwhelmingly God-Centered, God-Driven, God-Inspired! We could—we just might—we prayed together to be instruments of God's Peace.

It is our most constant prayer and the culmination and unexpected gift of our *entire* journey.

> God of all the World!
> Fill us with your Presence and your Peace.
> Help us work together to know you,
> And to love you,
> And to listen to your voice above the noise of a fractured world!
>
> Heal us all,
> Hold us in your loving care,
> Help us join together to bring Peace to Your World.
>
> Amen.

CHAPTER 34

An Unexpected Visual Of God

God in a dream picture.

In all of the richness, color, joy and excitement of everything that was happening to us though our study and the subsequent programs it contained, I had a dream that was really a picture of God.

In my dream was a single object. The entire space was filled with an enormous tree, each branch so filled with leaves that you could scarcely see anything else. A little sky shown through the richly thickened branches and leaves; but there was nothing else except this living, breathing tree!

I stood before the tree and observed all its branches and every leaf. It was so immense I felt there was never a tree made like it in the whole world. I knew its root system must go deep into the earth to draw upon the water necessary to feed this marvelous creation.

It was in full bloom, its leaves a deep green, its bark a thickened brown. There was life in this tree: strength, power, permanence. There was peace in this tree: welcoming, comforting, protecting. I could see neither the top nor the bottom of the tree. But I knew its branches stretched far into the sky and its roots deep into the ground.

I didn't touch the tree. I didn't wrap my arms around it, and even if I had wished to do so, the circumference of this mighty creation would have been far too large for me to contain.

I saw my tree as pure gift and a portrait of things past and things to come: A tree of the richness and color and splendor of God.

What more wonderful symbol than this marvelous representation of the power and beauty of life: this tree that filled every inch of space before me.

What more marvelous gift than to discover this living tree: to trust its origins and to experience its thick abundance, depth and permanence.

We are all a part of that magnificent tree, enclosed within its rich and welcoming space: one within our diversity; one within our connection to God.

That is the miracle and the meaning and the mystery that was unfolding in my life *every day.*

In Praise and Gratitude to God who brings us all into one connection!

Amen.

PART IV

GOD EVERYWHERE

"By (the Token of) Time (through the ages),
Verily Man is in loss,
Except such as have Faith, and do righteous deeds,
And join together in the mutual teaching of
Truth, and of Patience and Constancy."

From the Quran, Surat 103

"Compassionate Source of Healing,
Heal us and we shall be healed;
Save us and we shall be saved;
Grant us a perfect healing for all our infirmities."

Hebrew Text from the Weekday Evening Service

"I saw a new heaven and a new earth . . . and I heard a voice saying,
'Behold the dwelling of God is with all people . . . God will wipe away
every tear from their eyes, and death shall be no more . . . for the former
things have passed away . . . Behold I make all things new . . . I am the
Alpha and the Omega, the beginning and the end! To the thirsty
I will give water without price from the fountain of the water of life.'"

Excerpts from Revelations 21:1-7

CHAPTER 35

God In The Neighborhood

When God appears in neon lights you'd better pay attention!

We had recently moved to a third floor condo in a small business district. It suited our needs and the commercial neighborhood included a small grocery store, gas station, branch bank and a variety of other small stores to make life convenient and interesting.

The trouble was that about half stores were unoccupied, which meant the neighborhood was in a deep decline. Everyone recognized the situation but no one knew how to fix it. I was aware, but didn't know what I could do either until one night . . .

I was looking out our dining room windows overlooking the street. It was deserted except for a few cars coming home for the night. Most of the stores locked their doors at 6:00, but kept some lights in the windows.

It was almost, but not quite dark. I stood at the windows, observing the neighborhood, not thinking much about anything at all. And then . . .

I saw three large letters, in blazing neon lights, suspended outside our windows. I shook my head to make sure I wasn't seeing things. But they were still there: three large flashing neon letters which formed a word that didn't make any sense.

I looked again—they were still there, so large I couldn't miss them. The letters spelled the word: NAG!

Since I wasn't feeling petulant or out of sorts, I didn't think it referred to me. But why in the world was the word "NAG" hanging outside our dining room windows? It didn't make any sense—until I suddenly saw the word NAG as an acronym for something else. N-A-G must have another meaning.

As the neon letters kept flashing, I kept thinking about possible options until suddenly everything fell into place: NAG must stand for "*Neighborhood Action Group*" which was precisely what this neighborhood needed to return to life.

I smiled, knowing there was only one explanation for this bizarre happening. God must be around somewhere in the neighborhood, offering a direct solution to our problem. And if that sounds crazy to you, it seemed pretty strange to me too, except I'd grown accustomed to having God appear anywhere and everywhere and always with the same agenda: *New Life*.

And new life was exactly what this neighborhood needed to survive! So why not a *Neighborhood Action Group* to bring new life and new stores into our dying neighborhood Creativity always needs a starting place where it can unfold its gifts! NAG was exactly the right way to go about the job.

The next part was obvious. Our neighborhood action group, NAG for short, needed to have some members! Why not ask the merchants in the area and the people living in the neighborhood to become part of a team effort to bring new life and new businesses to our street. All I had to do was ask. The next day I took a pad of paper and pen and canvassed a few stores in the neighborhood with a simple question: "Would you like to join NAG, our neighborhood action group, to help bring new life to the neighborhood?" Six stores signed up immediately.

The following day, my solicitation continued with the rest of the occupied stores and every one joined. Each day, I reached out to the merchants and neighbors living and working in the area. Within a very few weeks we had over 200 names on our NAG list. The name was pure magic.

Merchants were definitely interested in any means to NAG the local government for not helping to revitalize our neighborhood. Home and Condo owners wanted to NAG the same group for the same and more reasons. The local government heard about us and immediately became suspicious that we were subversive and out to do no good.

The candidate for Village Manager in the next election came to see me to try to get NAG to vote for him.

The miracle was in the name. Belonging to an organization called NAG made everyone smile! Nagging turned out to be a very good idea, whether anyone carried it out or not. It was a benign way to express anger and frustration without creating any real damage.

Being too many in number to meet in any neighborhood location, I kept us in regular connection through email and snail mail. For those with electronic connections, email was a natural. For those older residents in our neighborhood, who didn't or weren't able to do email, I did a printout of our emails and delivered them in person.

When you deliver mail in person, you get to say hello and get a hug. It increases Spirit geometrically.

Our numbers grew. So did the good feelings in the neighborhood. I began to see us as being on a *"spiritual mission"*. I even shared my blinking neon light story and no one seemed to think it was crazy or weird. We had become a *virtual group* that never met, but had a powerful mission to revitalize our neighborhood!

Soon new stores began to arrive on the scene. We helped one new owner get a parking permit for his coffee shop by appearing at the local permit meeting. We held a concert at the small park in the neighborhood with a band named "Jeanie and the Jelly Beans", a soft rock group especially geared for families. We learned historical facts about the buildings in the area, some of which were landmark properties. We learned to *love* our neighborhood as the valued place it was becoming for all of us.

We smiled at being *naggers* who had discovered that sometimes big things can happen with good will rather than animosity. I also thought about creating an organization called, "NAG International" to go on the road to other areas that needed "New Life". But I didn't go there this time. (Maybe someday in the future!)

When our empty stores were almost all filled, I knew it was time to disband our NAG organization. Our mission was accomplished; new life was all around us. Everyone was happy! Go out on a winner! Everyone could celebrate that.

In a special ribbon cutting ceremony, we gave the neighborhood a new name and NAG was put to rest. Greatly relieved to have NAG gone, our local government heaved a final sigh of relief. Life returned to normal!

How do I explain my neon lights outside my dining room windows on the third floor of our condo building?

I don't try because I *know* that God was somehow in the neighborhood helping us. And sometimes, God *is all mystery with no explanations*. And that is sufficient!

(It was also another reminder that sometimes God does seem to have a sense of humor in the middle of life's ongoing struggles!)

CHAPTER 36

God In Small Moments

Finding God in two transformed lives.

1. The phone rang. A familiar voice was on the other end. A clergy friend of mine often sent referrals to me, people in his church he thought would benefit from my services as a psychologist. Over the years we had become good friends and shared similar ideas about the healing process.

"I have someone I want you to see." Our conversations usually started with this opening.

"That's fine. I'd be happy to do that. What's going on?" He often supplied me with some introductory material so I'd hear his perspective on the situation. He was unusually understanding and well trained about psychological issues and I valued his input whenever it was available.

"Oh no," he interrupted, "This is not going to be a patient. There's a man in my congregation who wants to talk about spiritual matters. I told him you were the expert in that area, not me."

I smiled at the idea that my friend, with over forty years of experience and expertise in ministry, was sending someone to me for some form of spiritual information.

But he knew about the study. He also trusted that what I had to offer about spiritual matters was based on solid research and not some flimsy, inaccurate, untested ideas about God.

I gathered this would also be important to the man I was about to meet.

Sometime in the next few weeks, the phone rang and our connection was made. I heard an appropriate hesitation in his voice that seemed to be saying underneath his message: I'm not sure what I'm getting myself into. We made an appointment to meet at the church. But I scheduled it in the next few days in case he changed his mind.

When the day of our appointment came, our cars arrived at the church at about the same time, separated by a few other parked cars. I got a quick glimpse of his face as we both exited from our cars. If I had to put what I saw into words, I would start with "discomfort" and add something that looked like "pain".

I turned away quickly and walked into the church, not wanting to engage in a conversation before we got to a less public place.

We had agreed to meet in a room in the basement of the church that was used for board meetings. Comfortably furnished with a large conference table and about a dozen cushioned chairs, the room seemed too large for the intimacy of God talk. But it was also away from the busy-ness of the church in a silent room that promised privacy and neutrality. Those qualities would help.

We sat down at one end of the room. The chairs had wheels to provide the ability to move from a side by side position to one in which we could face each other. I had my first glimpse of his face at close range.

I knew immediately I could trust him. Words didn't provide that response. I was simply aware that this was an errand he was not doing lightly. Something important was going to happen and there was an urgency that was felt, though not spoken in words.

We started to talk in small increments of information. We both knew *how* he had found me. But the truth was he really didn't know *why* he had come. Silence between expressed thoughts wasn't uncomfortable. But I knew something more was waiting to happen.

I listened to the shared words being aware that part of me was also listening for something else. It was as if I were in two scenes in this one setting.

Time passed; more information given. The dividing line between therapy and spiritual conversation is very clear. We were not there to talk about personal problems. We were there to talk about Spirit, but not as information to be discussed. Spirit doesn't work that way.

Without thinking or making a rational decision, I reached out, took his hands into my hands and said simply, "Let's pray." I was responding to an inner sense of the need for connection between us and with God.

I watched his face as I took his hands. I had not asked permission to pray and I could see his discomfort. Praying was not part of the expected outcome.

But I knew that God was in the room with us. Praying was the opening of that door for me and for us. If my friend's discomfort forced him to leave, God would certainly "stir" the waters again for him in another time and place. If he chose to stay, a door would open that would change *both* of our lives.

The moment had come for God to become *real* in our situation. Praying steps past all the usual ways we try to avoid God. Praying with hands joined brings the reality of what we are doing into full view. The words are not nearly as important as the realization that we are acknowledging God *with* us: the first step in an incredible journey of new life.

The moment had come. My new friend looked carefully at me for a very long moment. Not taking his hands away, he breathed a quiet sigh, re-settled into his chair—and he stayed.

And so did God! We had begun our new journey together.

II. John was a patient in my practice as a psychologist. He came to me with a disturbed marriage, no children and the need to change his life.

Then he contracted a serious disease that was potentially fatal. He was in his early forties.

John was spiritually motivated and educated. He was also deeply knowledgeable about music, although not a musician. He was sensitive, caring and surprisingly not distraught about his illness.

It somehow fit into his life at the time we first met.

We worked through some of the issues of his early family and his marriage. I met his wife and felt the separation they were both experiencing. The therapeutic work was quiet—an unusual word to use in describing our time together. But it had a peaceful quality to it and also held a spiritual awareness that was always there.

John sought medical help when he was first diagnosed with serious cancer. The medical community had various medications and treatments that would help to slow the progress of his disease. But no one suggested that he could be cured.

He talked about his options with me and then did his own reflections away from our sessions to make a decision as to his future health strategies. He chose to refuse treatments of any kind. We spoke about the why's of his decision. Was he so depressed that he needed medication to make a different decision? He didn't believe that was the case and he didn't show symptoms of serious depression.

We spoke about the impact of his decision on his wife and his parents. But he and his wife had already reached a point of no return and were going to separate. His parents accorded him the right to choose what he wanted from his life.

We talked about the progression of his disease. What would he do when intolerable pain became a part of his life? He was able to process all these questions and come to the same conclusion. His life was in God's hands. He had no hesitation in choosing this pathway. It was part of his belief system to know that God was actively engaged in the world and in his life. He didn't make a choice based on non-intervention in his disease as a religious principle.

He chose to live out his life within a strong belief that God was with him in the process and would be with him at the end of his life as well. I chose to accompany him on his spiritual journey. Our therapeutic relationship became a friendship with God and both of us.

As his pain mounted, he finally needed to be hospitalized. The medical community did not approve of his choice: their passion is to help and cure people. But they agreed to find a small room for him, in a quiet section of the hospital and provide whatever relief he would permit.

I continued to visit with him at the hospital. Our conversations were quiet moments talking about God, and were surprisingly peaceful. His room was actually quite isolated so the usual sounds and activity of the hospital were nearly absent.

It was only a matter of a few weeks until we both knew his dying was getting close. He called his parents and they arrived to be with him. He shared the plans he had made for his final moments. He wanted our time of prayer and connection to start the completion of his life. Then he wanted time with his parents without my being there. In their private goodbye, he wanted them to listen to Mahler's Resurrection Symphony together.

I left him in a peaceful place with God filling the room. The experience of his dying had deeply touched me. I didn't know how to think about it or process it for myself.

When I got home, I sat and waited, still connected to John and his parents and God. An hour later, a phone call interrupted my silence. It was John's parents in joy and excitement as well as sorrow.

In the last moment of his life, just before he died, John suddenly smiled and said to them, "Call Bobbie. Tell her I made it!" We all knew what that meant.

He had transcended this world and arrived at the next! And he had found a way to share the gift with the three of us. In whatever way we can know these powerful transitions, we all understood he was now and forever with God. His life had moved on to the next destination in this journey we all share.

My heart said "thank you" to the God in whose presence he had found peace. After that, I felt the silence and the miracle of what we had just experienced. No words can contain the enormity of this profound passage from life into new life.

These transitions from death into a new, unknown moment remain a mystery to be revealed for each of us when the time comes for us to die. We cannot *know* until that time, and so we must finally *trust* that this unknown darkness also contains the Light. And it is this "darkness transformed into Light" that is the ultimate connection and final gift of a Loving God for each one of us.

In Thanks and Love to all who go before us.

In Gratitude and Praise to God who leads the way.

Amen.

CHAPTER 37

God In Another Parking Lot

The unexpected God who surprised me!

I was very angry. A clergy friend was being very badly treated by his congregation and righteous indignation rose up in me spilling out over everything that interrupted its path.

In that state of mind, I put on my walking shoes and hit the sidewalks with a vengeance. Mechanically I followed my usual walking route which takes me past the Baha'i Temple toward the lake. Ordinarily, I look forward to this daily walk that brings me into direct contact with one of the world's most beautiful places.

The Temple is the central location of the Baha'i Faith in the Western Hemisphere. It is stunningly beautiful, rising up majestically from the street, surrounded with incredible gardens and fountains.

Inside is a beautiful large open space seating hundreds of worshippers and visitors. Simply furnished with chairs, it invites one to a quiet space to visit and contemplate God from whatever faith perspective one holds.

Worship is led by a reader in front, with a simple table for resources, a microphone and flowers on either side. Sayings from the Baha'i Faith are imprinted on both the inside and the outside walls: marvelous expressions of the Depth, Mystery and Spirit of their faith.

REVEREND BOBBIE MCKAY, PH.D.

But on this day, when I was walking on the sidewalk outside the Temple Gardens, I was determined that nothing spiritual would interrupt my frame of mind. However, I did not count on God.

I was so engrossed in my own situation that I didn't see that the parking lot at the Temple was filling up with cars. I didn't even notice the heavier than usual traffic on the street. I rounded the corner of the Temple and a crossing street and ran right into one of the policemen that patrolled the Temple at night.

He started to talk with me in a pleasant, encouraging way, but his words were totally unexpected. "You need to hear this concert!" Looking up at him, I didn't know what he was talking about. He continued: "This is a wonderful concert. You need to hear it," with the emphasis on the words "you" and "need". I still didn't quite get it.

One more time he spoke. "This concert today—you need to hear it."

"What concert?" the words stumbled out.

"The concert they're having today, right here at the Temple. There are one hundred people in the chorus and they've already done a standing room only concert this morning."

I must have looked a bit confused. He came closer and said. "Let me help you. Do you live in the neighborhood or close by? I'll save a place for you in the parking lot so you can be sure to get a seat at the concert."

My angry state was finally interrupted sufficiently for me to respond to this obviously very kind policeman who was making extraordinary efforts to reach through my angry barriers. My words stumbled out in his direction. "I need to get in touch with my husband so he can hear the concert too. We live a few blocks up this street." I pointed out the direction to where we live.

My new policeman friend said, "Let me take you on a shortcut that will help you get home more quickly." He took my hand, walked me into the lower level of the Temple, which led directly to an exit where I could reach home in a shorter amount of time.

As we parted company, he added, "I'll be waiting for you in the parking lot with your own saved parking place. But be sure to hurry." He smiled and disappeared.

As soon as I got outside, I remembered I didn't have to run home—I had my cell phone with me. I called Lew and said to him, "There's a concert at the Baha'i Temple and we have to hear it." Lew had been asleep and what I said wasn't connecting very well.

"There's a concert at the Temple and we have to hear it. Get in the car and drive down here . . . a policeman is holding a space in the parking lot."

Shaking off the dis-connect of sleep, he finally said "OK if you want, I'll drive down."

The traffic was getting much heavier. I worried about my policeman friend waiting in the parking lot. My anger had completely disappeared in the urgency of hearing this concert.

Finally, Lew arrived. Thanks to our helping friend, we had a parking place immediately adjacent to the entrance to the parking lot. We hurried across the street, and found seats in the Temple just before the concert started. My excitement grew as we saw the program with one hundred names listed and the amazing range of music being presented.

The choir came down two side aisles, dressed in quiet black. People from all over the world had come to sing in this concert. The director was waiting as they processed to their place of performance. When they were ready, he lifted his arms and they began to sing in perfect unison, with no pitch provided. It was as if the opening notes were somehow imprinted in their musical memory.

For two hours, they sang of God, Life, Joy, Happiness, Sorrow and Spirit in music from faith communities and traditions around the world. It was done without instrumentation of any kind. The interplay of one hundred voices and their Director became a perfect musical image of the direct inter-connectedness of God and all of God's people.

I sat quietly listening to every note, every word. I knew I was in the Presence of God who was providing me with another entry point into my own spirit through the miracle of music and words. Music enters our hearing, finds its way to the brain through the heart and then extends itself into every fiber of Spirit within the body.

One song, toward the end of the concert, especially caught my attention. It had a repeated phrase that echoed over and over again as if to make sure that it was recognized and retained.

The melody was simple. The words kept repeating:

"I opened my Mouth to the Lord, and I won't go back."

There was a strong rhythmic quality to the phrase that punctuated every word.

"I opened my Mouth to the Lord, and I won't go back."

It spoke to me of the power of our God connection. Once we *take in* the presence of God, we won't go back . . . we *can't* go back to our former state of emptiness. God has filled us and become a permanent part of us. We are a new creation. There is no going back to former times.

I might try to ignore that presence, as I had done in my anger earlier that day, and as all of us do when we try to distance ourselves from God. Or when I'm in my stubborn resistant mode and I don't want to hear something or I don't want to do something, I can go to great lengths to try to avoid God.

But once we have opened ourselves to the Presence and Reality of God, we truly cannot go back to where we were before. We can interrupt the journey or deviate from the path. But the road has been set and we are on it. God is ever faithful and we're not on trial. Whenever I am lost and separated, all I have to do is to take in a deep breath, "open my mouth to the Lord", and be reminded of our connection.

I can also remember a policeman who told me I had to hear the concert (which I did); took me by the hand to show me a short cut through the lower level of the Temple (into my spirit) and saved a parking place so we wouldn't miss a single moment of the music.

After the concert, we tried to find the policeman to thank him. But he wasn't anywhere to be found. And like our map friend when we were gathering data on the road from Philadelphia to Baltimore on Highway 95, closer to Baltimore than Philadelphia, all our efforts to find him failed.

But my never-to-be-forgotten encounter with the mystery of God had already taken place.

Praise and Thanks to the always present God who manages to find us anywhere and everywhere, especially when we are "lost".

Blessed are they who lead us into God territory.

Blessed are we when we can recognize God and follow.

Blessed are those who supply us with the Music of God's Everlasting Love and Presence.

Blessed are the peacemakers who lead us into new life.

Amen and Amen!

CHAPTER 38

God And The "Boomers"

The country's largest cohort discovers God.

Our Baby Boomers have not only come of age, they are entering old age by the thousands. Born between 1946 and 1964, they are now ages 49 to 67 and definitely moving into the middle and later years of their lives.

In the data from our research we found amazing information about spiritual life across the entire life cycle. Part of the data was quite intriguing. We asked people at what age or ages they experienced the presence of God in their lives, as *they understood God*. We didn't offer arbitrary time frames or suggestions to bias their answers.

According to the people who participated in our study and filled out our questionnaire, the peak number of God experiences occurred around age 48. After sixty, the number of God experiences began to decline.

We were surprised by this finding. Why was God appearing more at age 48 than at other ages?

Why not God in our older years? A few people reported experiences of God in their childhood or adolescence; a few more experienced God in their early adulthood with slight increases through their 30's and early 40's

But around age 48, God seems to arrive precisely at a time when all of life is bursting with activity. Forty eight and the years on either side are pandemonium: heavy responsibilities, children, aging parents, competition for advancement; first signs of an aging body; and beginning questions about meaning and mortality. A huge agenda!

Forty Eight leads to fifty which is just ten years from sixty. It *is* a midpoint in life; a bridge to cross into the first years of early old age. An upward spiral begins to peak and start its return on a descending curve!

In an additional study we did on spiritual life over the age of sixty, we learned from many people in their 70's and 80's that *survival issues* usually take precedence over spiritual issues in old age. Questions like: Will I have enough money for my old age? If I don't have the money I need, who will take care of me? Will I be alone and have to take care of myself? How will I die? Will it be painful? Will my family take care of me? Will I outlive my friends? Where will I live? What will happen to me after my death?

We found very few *spiritual* questions or answers on that list.

Later, listening to a chaplain at a retirement home near us, we heard a different viewpoint about aging. He smiled when we talked about our data and then shared unexpected conclusions from his experience and understanding. "If you don't find God in your 30's, you'll never make it in old age!"

In your thirties! We couldn't believe our ears. But he was quite serious. "Aging is so difficult, it carries such heavy duty problems, it is so unpredictable, and people age so differently that you have to be prepared for anything that might happen. The time for that preparation is in your thirties before those busy years in your forties and fifties and the onslaught of aging in your sixties."

There was something very compelling about his argument. What he was essentially saying is that being grounded in God in our thirties ensures that nothing can shake that spiritual anchoring when the inevitable changes and issues of aging enter our lives later! Whatever our childhood ideas and fantasies of God are about, we need to discover an *adult version* of God before we reach old age.

Meanwhile, our mid-fifties are often times when the winds of change start to re-enter our lives. We feel them as a kind of beginning discontent and dissatisfaction with the way life is going and what our future appears to be. Sometimes it's expressed in that critical question: Is this all there is to life?

It appeared that three issues might be happening concurrently in this powerful mid-life time: a beginning awareness of change in my life; the first glimpse of what old age might look like—all set in the context of growing responsibilities and an increasing number of God experiences. An amazing agenda that would not go away!

Our Baby Boomers are standing on that powerful edge of *life until I die* or *new life and spirit* while *I* am still very much alive. This is the first generation that has had the opportunity to look at these issues in a brand new context.

It used to be that by the time we reached fifty, our lives were pretty much settled and we could look forward to a retirement in our mid-sixties. But all that has changed and forty eight is no longer too old to take on something new and run with it. Expressions like: Seventy is the new fifty; eighty is the new sixty tell the story of a changing life cycle with the "Boomers" leading the way with their insistence on the continuation of life beyond existing limits.

The critical issue is being able to recognize God in this process, expanding it to include new *spiritual* directions in mid-life, which will *automatically* enrich your old age.

Rumor has it the "Boomers" intend to live a very long life and don't really expect to die. People often treat that conviction with some mockery and disdain. But perhaps our enormous supply of Baby Boomers are wise enough to know that Spirit never dies. They work hard to keep their bodies in shape and their minds actively engaged in the world to ward off some of the restrictions of physical and mental aging. Perhaps a generous God is also providing an opportunity to recharge their spirits as well as their bodies and mind.

Spirit doesn't age. It only gets better. Our mid-life experiences with God are creating an environment of new life and energy: new reasons to live to carry us through the rest of our lives, if we pay attention to the latest intersections of God in the world.

The central message of our adult life is to *get ready*. Spiritual growth even into our one hundred's is no longer unusual. Our bodies may age, but our spirits can still fly! Hang on to God and the journey will take you where you never dreamed you'd be.

But remember: God's other name is Surprise! Close no options and keep your heart and spirit open to new opportunities and new life whenever you see them. You can always recognize God by the excitement and the passion you feel, no matter how chronologically old you happen to be.

Once again, God's signature of *New Life* can lead the way to an unbelievably satisfying old age, filled with the wisdom and joy of having still found God at the center of everything.

Finally the way is cleared for us to return Love for Love and Life for Life.

Praise God for these astonishing gifts that just keep on growing!

Amen.

CHAPTER 39

God Never Leaves Loose Ends.

A Four version opera is completed.

Periodically, in this amazing journey with God, I'd write another musical and be reminded of the first gift that God brought into my life after my original experience of God in my dining room. The piano was always an immediate source of beauty and harmony that simply grew even though there was little time for it.

However, one day Lew said, "How'd you like to write the music for an opera? I have an idea for an Epiphany opera . . . a story about Melchior, one of the Wise Men, who saw the Christ Child and his life was entirely transformed by the experience. Then he had to go home and explain his transformation to his wife and child."

We both liked the idea. Lew's words became a special story which I set to music. The opera was still incomplete, but a good start. (Version 1).

A few years later, we went back to the opera with some revisions and a partial new ending. (Version 2).

Several years later, we revived the opera, fixed the ending (we thought) and found a friend with musical expertise to listen to the score. He said simply, "It's not finished." We knew he was right, but didn't want to know it. (Version 3).

About five years later, I said to Lew, "If we don't finish the opera soon, we'll be dead. It's time!"

Then I suddenly realized that our opera was exactly the same story we were hearing in our research. What happens when we encounter God? How does that transforming experience change our lives? And what impact does it have on the lives of the people around us?

We couldn't write a proper ending until we realized the connection between what we were living (doing the research) and the story we were creating. They were exactly the same, except that our research didn't cover the effect of our spiritual transformation on the people who are intimately involved with us. And neither did our opera.

Enter God—who was really there all the time. We drastically changed the ending, I added some new songs having to do with the impact of transformation on everyone, especially the wise man's wife, and their relationship. The opera became complete and was performed in a concert version in 2008. (Version 4).

Initially, our cast of eight graduate music students from Northwestern University were rather casual about the story, concentrating on learning the music. After the performance was over, they all said their lives had been changed in very meaningful ways by performing the opera. An unexpected new group was learning about God.

God is ever patient, and always persistent. Sometimes we are living in the middle of a process, but miss seeing a critical element that changes everything. In our case, we were engaged in powerful research about transformation and its effect on the individual being "transformed", but had not yet investigated the impact of that change on the people around them.

Solving that problem in our research would mean talking to friends, spouses, co-workers, and family members of people transformed by their God experiences to see the impact on *their* lives: an exciting new direction to explore of the impact of God in the world.

In our opera, it meant my writing two new songs: one for Melchior's wife about *her* transformation and one for both of them to sing together of the changes in each of their lives as a result of Melchior's encounter with the Christ child.

The *opera* had become an unexpected, stimulus in our research. The *research* opened a door to a new ending for our opera. Two non-related happenings in our lives were suddenly linked by the spiritual changes it was creating in everyone involved.

Whenever we encounter God, the impact deeply affects the people around us. It can open God's door for them as well and has the potential to change everything—for everyone.

> More learning, more God!
> More wonder and more awe.
> More Praise and more Thanks!
>
> More celebration of God's infinite Presence in everything in Life!
> More excitement and joy that God is so actively engaged with
> our world!
> More thanks for the miracle of Music.
>
> And no more loose ends!

CHAPTER 40

God Is Not A Causal Agent

Knowing what God is and is not is critical.

Often people will decide that God is actually a causal agent directly linked to our behavior. If I am very good, God will give me what I want; and its corollary: God will punish those who are not very "good".

This is a fundamental misconception of the nature of God. The nature of God is God's "Is-ness". God Is; God exists; God's Presence is God's Promise to be with us. God's reality is manifest in "New Life".

We know these truths through the writings of multiple faith traditions and all the millions of individuals who have experienced God in their lives. When we attribute causality to God, connecting our behaviors to God's activities, we deeply diminish God and live within a set of rules that *people* have created, not God.

God is Presence; God is Mystery. We can't explain God no matter how much wisdom we hold. Our relationship with God is all about New Life in whatever circumstances we are living.

Most of us live pretty honest, caring lives. We know the rules and we abide by them. We teach our children and our grandchildren those rules by the way we live them. It's not very complicated. We're not interested in hurting people nor in having other people injure us. We try to live with honesty and integrity. We're not living like characters in a television drama engaged in destructive behaviors toward self or others.

When we recognize God in our lives, we begin a new life with God at the center. New Life means knowing something of the Mystery and Presence of God. New Life means new opportunities for living our lives with more depth and meaning and *seeing* more of God in my life whenever I open my eyes to look for God. New life does not mean controlling God's response with my behaviors, no matter how *good* they may seem.

One of the most physically painful experiences in my life came after I had a badly botched back surgery. Apparently I am unaffected by pain medications. In that time of nearly unbearable pain, I was suddenly aware of a growing depth in my spiritual life. It was if my physical pain and my spiritual life stood side by side, different entities in my being that were suddenly exposed. My pain wasn't diminished, but my spirit was growing.

Did God *cause* my botched surgery? Of course not! Years ago people might have seen that as *punishment* for something bad I had done. But we don't live in a causal relationship with God where we control God with our behaviors, good or bad. My physicality was simply unmoved by medications that diminish pain for most people.

But God's spirit, experienced *within* my pain, was healing my life.

In our study, people often discovered God in the darkest places of their lives, not making things better, but being Present and by that Presence creating New Life. Many people described feelings of gratitude for deeply painful times as unforgettable learning lessons. Jobs lost, children injured, finances destroyed, death of loved ones—all turned out to be opportunities to discover this fundamental connection between God and life.

GOD IS NEW LIFE and that means within every situation exists the opportunity for an emerging new life: the decision to "live" or to "die": to give up or continue; to learn new lessons or to be buried in the old ways. We can have death or we can have resurrection. God has given us the choice.

God didn't rescue Jesus, but out of Jesus' death came Jesus' resurrection.

When the old, familiar ways turn out to be inappropriate or impossible, we are presented with the opportunity to transpose that situation into a different pattern of behavior.

But sometimes in our despair, when life doesn't seem to be getting any better for us, we may turn to judge other people's lives and see *them* as deserving of the trouble they're having. Or we wonder why God doesn't punish bad people who do terrible things.

One of the participants in our research was a young African American minister whose brother had been shot and killed for no apparent reason—an innocent victim in a crime that had nothing to do with him. Our young minister shared his pain and his anger and the fact that he simply couldn't forgive the killer.

It had begun to eat away at him that he was a minister who was supposed to forgive and forget and he could do neither.

Finally he decided to visit the man who killed his brother and was now incarcerated for the crime. He needed to ask him one question: Why? Why did he commit this terrible crime? Not to know the *why* was killing him.

It was easy enough to arrange the visit since clergy are usually welcome at prisons. When he sat down with his brother's killer and was able to look directly at him, he said, "Why? Why did you do that? Why did you kill my brother?"

He stopped for a moment, caught his breath and then continued. "The man couldn't answer my question. But he asked me for my forgiveness. And somehow, it allowed me to feel healed. But my family is *not* healed yet."

We don't always know "why" something happens. God remains both Mystery and Presence. Sometimes there are no explanations.

In all circumstances, and especially in life's worst tragedies, the only door that can open for us is the one that moves us toward *new life*. In fact, it is within these terrible tragedies that we are sometimes enabled to see new life emerging.

God was present to our clergy friend's brother in his death as well as the one who killed him. God was present to me even when my pain was unrelenting and nearly unbearable. Even when we don't see it, or don't *want* to see it, the gift of new life is always waiting for us to open our eyes to see God.

> God is not a magician who alters life with special magic.
> God is not a powerful ruler who controls us through our acceptable behaviors.
> God is not our personal property which can be "bought" for a price.
> God is not retribution for wrongs committed or lives destroyed.
>
> God is Presence; New Life; Love; Mystery; Passion and Spirit that permeate the entire world. We can access God in any moment by knowing that God is right here, right now.
>
> We can see it or not. We can turn away this time and return the next.
> We can question, doubt, be afraid, get angry!
> It doesn't matter.

But if we choose to see God, the terrible depths of pain and sorrow can begin the healing process of new life. It is not so much an issue of *trusting* God, but rather *knowing* that God is that direction toward New Life that will ultimately heal us, whenever we can release our hold on *our* insistence of life's outcomes, no matter what.

"Let go and let God" is a strategy that brings us into a brand new territory of possibilities available only when we let go of our control. It is a fundamental truth for millions of people in Alcoholics Anonymous and other Twelve Step Programs. But it applies to all of us who would discover new life emerging from the depths of our pain and sorrow.

A version of that truth was sent to me in a photograph of an old mail truck where someone had written these words in large letters across the dusty, very dirty side door: "TRY GOD!"

Indeed!

Let us try God whenever life turns on us;

Let us try God whenever we don't know where to go;

Let us try God when we have lost hope or courage;

Let us try God when all doors seem closed!

And Find God Waiting.

Amen.

CHAPTER 41

God In Two "Miracles"

The unexpected gifts!

I. Unexpectedly, I was in sudden intense pain, with no apparent cause, in the upper right quadrant of my back. X-rays at an outpatient clinic didn't explain the pain which only worsened. Calling my doctor on a Saturday seemed hopeless because most doctors are unavailable on the weekends. But pain won out and amazingly I reached him at the local hospital.

"Come on over and let me look at you. It might just be better to have you go into the hospital to get some MRI's. Easier to get whatever tests we need right here in the hospital."

By this time I had lost my ability to raise my right arm and was more than willing to find out what was wrong. We ran tests and came up with a diagnosis of brachial plexus, a convergence of nerves causing terrible pain, and the problem of raising my arm. Over time, with physical therapy it would get better. After two days of tests, I was ready to leave the hospital.

The moment I got home, there was an urgent call waiting from my doctor! In order to be released from the hospital, a chest x-ray was required. In checking the results of the chest x-ray, they found a tumor in my lungs. I needed more tests and surgery to determine the nature of the tumor. It was removed immediately along with one third of my lung for preventive measures.

The tumor was malignant, and the question of lymph node involvement remained. We would know within three days of the surgery. The unexpectedness of the diagnosis had taken us completely by surprise. It was a few days before Christmas and a three day wait seemed unbearable.

On the *first* night after the surgery, we were anxiously talking in my hospital room. It was around 9:00 p.m. when the door suddenly opened and my surgeon appeared. He was dressed, not in the usual hospital garb, but an elegant suit and tie. And he was smiling.

"I just wanted to tell you the good news so you didn't have to wait any longer." He had been at a dinner party when the results of my tests were forwarded to him . . . two days early! The lung cancer was contained and no lymph nodes were involved.

He left the dinner party as soon as he received the news to come directly to the hospital to tell us. I think he was as relieved as we were. We will never forget seeing him in the doorway, as if God had come in person to share the good news.

In this kind of situation, it's not unusual to consider all the *what if's*. What if I hadn't experienced that sudden, intense pain in the right upper quadrant of my back and sought medical help? What if I hadn't seen the doctor on a no-appointment Saturday and not entered the hospital? What if the hospital had not required an x-ray to be discharged? We'd probably not have found this cancer until it was too late. Lung cancer is particularly virulent and I had no symptoms at all.

When we ask the parallel *why* questions we raise the issue of miracles. So called miracles, as they occur in life, don't lend themselves to factual explanations and controlled results. Some people have a terrible disease and get better. Others have a mild disease and don't survive. Too many variables are operating at any one time in the scientific world where *whys* can't always provide the correct answers. When you add the word *miracle,* you enter a different world.

The word *miracle* is complicated. For some, the word can become an occasion when God *chooses* to act or an occasion when God chooses *not* to act. If that is true, then when and under what conditions *does* God act? And why me, and not someone else!

But God can never be contained within a limited structure that acknowledges God when *good* things happen; and disavows God when they don't.

For me, miracles are always occasions of *new life*: unexplainable and *not tied to physical results*. The Mystery and Presence of God *is* the miracle, *whatever the outcome*. People in our study experienced a *miracle* when someone's fatal disease became the occasion for a family's healing. A doctor whose patient died spoke of the *miracle* of this experience through the shared dying process. The healing of the Spirit, without the curing of a disease, *is* a powerful miracle for any who have experienced it.

We live in a state of not knowing what will happen, no matter how careful we are. Life is unpredictable and we cannot know the future. But terrible tragedies often precede unexpected outcomes that are ultimately life changing. We don't know that until they become a reality.

The only way for life to be tolerable under those conditions is to live it as responsibly as we can, both for ourselves and for those whose lives intersect with or depend on ours. And to know, with as much certainty as we can find, that we are surrounded by a Presence and a Mystery that is both life giving and loving. Unfolding new life is the gift that follows whenever we allow ourselves to enter into the mystery and be transformed by it.

Healing and Curing are different entities. Curing is a gift of our human knowledge. Healing brings us into God's territory. And Healing always contains the gift of God Present and new life.

II. Our second miracle happened just two months ago. We were traveling on highway 80/90 in Ohio on our way to a grandson's graduation in Boston. This was a special journey of love and family: the opportunity to gather to celebrate the excitement of college completed and the future beyond school.

Everyone was driving around 80 MPH. The road was crowded, but the day was clear. In the next lane to our right was a flat—bed truck with a piece of four by eight, three quarter inch plywood in the back. Without warning, the plywood, which was not secured, was picked up by the wind, turned on its side and crashed into our windshield, arriving precisely between us, and shattering glass all over us.

Lew managed to brake and get us to the left side of the road. We sat in the middle of the shattered glass which covered both the front and the back seat, trying to catch our breath and take in what had happened. (Later we would discover the impact had been so powerful the glass had even entered the trunk.)

The windshield was completely shattered, the roof badly damaged, the plywood had broken the windshield, but miraculously the membrane in the windshield had held. Lew felt he had to get us over to the right side of the road for the necessary emergency vehicles to reach us. Waiting until we could get a clear shot across the highway, and trying to see through the side windows because there was no visibility through the windshield, the traffic finally cleared and we got across the road and stopped.

Meanwhile, the truck driver had parked and walked back to where we were sitting. Taking one look at these two older people, quietly sitting in shattered glass with seat belts still on, he called the police, the ambulance and his insurance company.

Miraculously, we walked away from the accident, were released from the hospital, arranged to have our car repaired, rented a car and continued on our way to Boston and the graduation.

Later we would talk about the *miracle* we had just experienced: the plywood that had come through the windshield *precisely* between us; the membrane in the windshield that had held through such a powerful impact; the fact that when Lew pressed the brakes to stop there were no cars behind us to cause a multiple car collision; the reality that Lew had been able to cross this very busy highway without a proper view of the road, made possible by the fact that there were no other cars in the vicinity. The amazing fact that the shattered glass that covered us and the front seat had not cut us.

We felt *God's Presence* in the entire experience.

And the *Mystery* continued in the next questions: Why weren't we seriously injured? How did we survive? As everyone told us how lucky we were, I thought about what it meant that we were actually able to continue our journey to honor our grandson's graduation. His response was one of deep gratitude that we had wanted to be there with him and not return to the safety of our home. Our grown children hoped it would convince us to fly instead of drive.

Friends talked of God and miracles.

What the accident said to both of us was that we were not quite finished with the work we had to do for God and that we had been given more time to continue what we had begun. What it said, specifically to me, was that it was time for me to write *this book . . . right now.*

We don't know what life is going to present to us. We can't predict the future with any certainty. Life interrupts our plans; interferes with our lives; changes our hopes and dreams; presents us with unwanted problems and sometimes dangerous situations. We have to live within this strange mix of uncertainty: not knowing what, when and where something might come to interfere with our living in this world.

Into that reality of *not knowing* comes the constancy of God: ever present, in the moment, and always available, not necessarily protecting us, but being with us. For those who have experienced God's Presence, these are words that hold deep meaning.

But for those who have not yet experienced God in any meaningful way, these words are difficult to grasp and understand. How does that work if all God does is to be present? What good is that anyway? And if we continue to look to God to give us what *we* decide we want or need, then we will always be disappointed in a God that is *only* Presence and Mystery.

But if we can search through our lives for a time when a *"no"* clarified our life; when an unexpected door opened for us that changed our future; when an anticipated loss was accompanied by a new discovery; when a word spoken changed our attitude. When something we saw, or read or heard caused us to rethink a situation; when an unexpected phone call brought us into contact with someone who cared about us.

When a loss turned out to be a gain.

When God walked into the dining room and changed my life.

When a man named Jesus was crucified, dead and buried and resurrected into new life.

God is Presence: known through the actions of other people and experiences with God.

God is Mystery: to enable us to look for God in the unexpected places in life.

God is New Life: to begin again.

My continual prayer is to remember that God is always around, contained in every moment.

> I can choose to stop and acknowledge God;
> Or I can turn away from God;
> I can know God's Presence
> Or I can refuse to see God

> Lord, Let me be quicker to see You ; to know You; to share You;
> and to love You with all of my being: all of my heart and
> all of my spirit.

In Praise and Thanksgiving!

Amen.

CHAPTER 42

A Different Kind Of "Miracle"

God at Kellogg School of Management, October, 2012

Miracles come in many sizes and shapes. This one came through a specific source *and* God. A wonderful new friend worked at Kellogg School of Management in their Executive Education Program. She thought we might learn from a new course they were teaching on "Essentials of Fund Raising and Marketing".

We have a small non-profit corporation and fund raising and marketing are essential for our survival and growth. We agreed it was a wonderful idea for us to take this class from a prestigious graduate school like Kellogg School of Management. A win-win for God and for us!

Receiving a generous scholarship for our class was our second God gift. Rich in gifts before we even started, we arrived early for our first class and were met with a lovely breakfast, lunch later and abundant food throughout the three days we met!

The next gift came when we discovered we were at least forty years older than most of the participants. It would be a challenge to listen to their experiences and strategies and see their responses to our research. We didn't know what to expect, but were exposed immediately to their energy and excitement. Our brains were fed with fabulous lectures, materials and new ideas in this complicated and amazing electronic world we inhabit. It was a powerful learning experience.

The final gift came at the end of our time together. "Graduation" was an opportunity to write a Brand for our product and share it with the class. In our case, the "product" was God. It was going to be a challenge. The others busied themselves in creative ideas for their Brands. Lew turned the assignment over to me and I prayed.

The brand that God and I created was immediate and very simple:

"DISCOVER GOD! SHARE THE GIFT.
CHANGE YOUR LIFE. CHANGE THE WORLD!"

Each participant's assignment was to share their Brands with everyone else: out loud! Any other information about their company was entirely welcome. As it turned out, I was the next to last person to speak, giving me more than enough time to get nervous.

As each person explained and read their brand, people responded with positive and affirmative comments and enthusiasm. I had determined not to read our Brand but that meant remembering it under stressful conditions. A new challenge!

My turn came. I stood up, took a deep breath and remembered every word. "Discover God; Share the Gift; Change your Life; Change the world!"

There was dead silence. No one spoke. An unexpected, uncomfortable quiet entered the room.

And then people started to clap and they continued to clap. A few cried. Encouragement was everywhere. And somewhere God had to be smiling.

And I discovered, in creating and speaking our new brand, it represented the whole truth from our study and everything we had done.

In all the years of doing research; talking with over 4000 people; traveling all over the country and in England; in making God our top priority; in spending twenty years of our lives in God's Service: It was all contained in those eleven words of our brand:

"Discover God! Share the Gift!
Change your Life! Change the World"

We discovered God in a highly successful learning institution for business and management in the heart of Chicago. We shared the Gift we'd been given. We issued the invitation to others to discover this life changing gift in their lives.

We had pronounced the truth as we had discovered it: This is how the world might be changed.

It can happen anywhere; everywhere; to anyone; anytime. God is a universal experience that knows no boundaries.

We have turned our brand into one hundred bumper stickers to go on the road! We hope you will see one and it will speak directly to your heart and spirit of God present in your life.

Please pass the message on to everyone you can.

With Thanks and Gratitude for this amazing journey,

Amen.

CHAPTER 43

God And Love

Getting to the Heart of God.

For most of my religious life, I've always understood that God was Love: Love expressed, Love given and Love received. One of the most famous scriptures in the New Testament carries the essence of that message:

> God so loved the world that he gave his only begotten son,
> That whosoever believed in him should not perish
> But have eternal life. John 3:16.

These words have been set to beautiful choral music and their message is visible in multitudes of paintings that exhibit God in a posture of Love toward the world.

Love surprises us both in the giving and receiving. We are surprised by the depth and breadth of love we carry around inside of us. Our love slips out in small hugs and smiles; it grows in moments when our heart opens to another person; it is particularly visible when we are around children, pets, and other vulnerable creatures. And it erupts in the passion for change we feel in causes and injustice and atrocities that happen in this world.

We can also experience God's love through other people who love us. Their care and their pleasure in being with us fills us with love. And when their love also insists on our growth and development, it gives us the chance to be fully human, fully spirit, fully connected to God and to the world.

One cannot measure love. It's like the constant beat of the heart. It happens without our causing it.

We don't *decide to love* someone or something. We discover that we *love* in a range of feelings awakened by persons and situations that touch us. There is no set pattern of who we are going to love. Love happens without our making it happen.

We can choose to *care* for someone and provide them with whatever they need to survive in this world. Caring can look a lot like love. But it isn't the same.

When we truly love someone, we learn that if circumstances called for such a sacrifice, we could give up our life for that person. It is the one gift that gives everything.

When my first grandchild was born, she was born prematurely: a beautiful, tiny girl, whose survival depended on her care in the infant intensive care unit of the hospital. Looking at her vulnerability, I first became aware of the passion I felt that she should live, no matter what it took.

In our daily visits to the hospital, I watched her struggle to survive, and that feeling grew in me. Her vulnerability awakened my spirit and strength to love with no conditions and to discover that Love and life are fully intertwined.

When we truly love someone, without conditions, love fills us and grows all the best in us as living, human beings. When that life is threatened, our connection grows. We want them to live because they and life are precious. When it is a vulnerable child, our love knows no boundaries.

I re-learned this lesson recently when I met with a group of people, talking about how special grandchildren are and how deeply touched we are by becoming a grandparent. Everyone had experiences to share about this amazing relationship of grandparents and grandchildren and powerful memories of life with great grandparents and their great grandchildren.

As I watched people talking, I saw the reflection of their words in their faces and bodies: Faces demonstrating the amazing reality of this special love in smiles and tears; bodies open, leaning forward to encompass this amazing love between the generations.

The gift was also seen in the reality that years had passed since those grandparents and great grandparents had died. And still the memory was activated into present time by the power of love remembered; love-given; love-received.

Years ago they used to place orphanages next to old people's homes to bring these generations together for mutual love and support. It was a special and very wise understanding of the link between the old and the young.

When I think of love, I think of my adult children and their children, our grandchildren, who reawaken in us such love and passion for life and for family.

When I think of love, I think of husbands and wives who have discovered, especially in their older years, how beautiful it is to be together in these final years of life.

When I think of love, I think of friends who continue to support and care for us, even when we are remiss in remembering.

When I think of love, I think of families and the struggles we face today to preserve those connections in a world of shifting jobs and locations and changing economic conditions.

When I think of love, I think of communities that that struggle to make life better for people in need and demonstrate love with concrete care and help.

When I think of love, I know that whenever I offer love, I am also the beneficiary of that gift. It is good for us to love.

When I think of love, I think of the thousands of people we have met through this amazing research study and its programs. Our lives have been so enriched by their presence that we have been transformed ourselves, over and over again.

When I think of love, I think of those moments when God has become so real in my life that I can feel and experience God's Presence as an opening to all of life, at all times and in all places.

When I think of Love, I think of all the connections we *could* be making to the people who share our planet. That kind of love means doing the hard work of acknowledging and connecting our differences; discovering our similarities of spirit; and, without the barriers of religious dogma, finding a way to work together in service and care.

When I think of Love, I look at all the pictures displayed in our home of our family, from their earliest days through the third generation of new families. I look at them with amazement and great anticipation for their future and the next generation to follow, with a dedicated determination that they shall all survive and grow.

When I think of Love, I think of "new Life" offered on a minute by minute basis by a God who seems committed to love us, no matter what we do to stifle or ignore that love.

When I think of Love, I am reminded that we are made in the image of God. Whatever opens our heart has some connection to the "heart" of God, constantly open to us.

This whole book has been a series of incidents in which God appears, in God's own way, to surprise us, inspire us and offer new pathways and people to grow our spirit. That God does not quit—or desert us is quite miraculous because we continue to look for ways to try to prove or disprove God's existence, and need to be continually reminded that God is right here—right now, waiting to connect.

When we discover the link between God and new life;

When we know and trust that God is both Presence and Mystery;

When we experience God's Presence in such a way that we KNOW God as a constant in our lives;

When we are able to share that knowledge and those experiences with other people;

Then the world around us will have a chance to live within the constancy of Spirit and new life,

And this book will have done its job.

CHAPTER 44

God And Lew

When God and Love enter together

Shortly after I began writing music, after my God experience in the dining room and the purchase of my piano, I was so filled with music that I volunteered to wrote a 90th anniversary musical for the church I belonged to.

It surprised me almost more than it surprised the people at the church. Who knew I could write music, let alone write full length musical?

But God is very persuasive and new life is rich in surprises. Everyone said "go for it" and I began to listen to the inner voice I had discovered that knew no boundaries as far as music was concerned.

The story, words, music and accompaniment simply unfolded into a package called, "The Story of Us", to be unveiled and produced in January, 1965.

Reality, however, was also a guest in the plan. Sensibility would dictate that I needed someone to direct this show if it were to be a success. I heeded the message and God intervened.

A few days later, I read in the local newspaper that a man named Lew Musil had just directed a musical for another religious community in the area. The timing was perfect; I found his phone number and called, anticipating a friendly response.

The response I got was short and immediate. "No. I'm not interested in directing a show right now". End of conversation.

Surprised and disappointed, but not dissuaded, I waited a few days and called him a second time. His words were identical. "No. I'm still not interested in directing a show right now."

Given my very real state of shyness and inexperience, one would think two negative replies would be sufficient to deter me from further action. However, one would be forgetting the arrival of God in my life and the power and energy it contained. I called him a third time.

Once again I requested his special skills as a director to help me produce this important musical event for our church. (He was also a member of the same church.)

The third time was either the charm or a weakened moment on his part or the hope that if he listened to my music it would be easy for him to be firm in his refusal. He agreed to come to my home and listen to the songs I had written.

Our house had a set of stairs leading from the sidewalk to the front porch and front door. At the set time for his arrival, I watched him from the window slowly walking across the sidewalk to the stairs.

If one could capture reluctance and resignation in a picture, he was the model for the scene. Head down, steps taken one at a time, putting off his arrival as long as possible, he ascended the steps, walked across the porch and rang the bell. The bell was musical with a chimed phrase that I let run its course. It delayed our meeting an extra few seconds.

Unable to avoid the moment any longer, he came in. Small talk was unnecessary. We had a task to accomplish, though we had separate anticipations. I knew the music was a gift from God and was appropriately beautiful. He knew anywhere else in the world would be preferable to being here.

I invited him to sit down and listen. For me to play and sing for a stranger who didn't want to listen was an occasion for terrible anxiety. I have an adequate voice but not one for public display. Still, it was a moment I couldn't avoid. Somehow I got through it and waited for his response.

He was quiet—that didn't reassure me. He didn't say anything for what seemed like five minutes. I regretted the whole thing. I couldn't even look to see if there were a positive response on his face.

It was the first time I had ever played and sung my songs for anyone else. Prior to this moment, they were part of my private spirit and life, not my public self. This was a moment that stopped time and space, as all such life changing moments always do.

I don't remember what Lew said. The words were out there, but they were caught up in that surround of fear, hope, joy and anxiety that filled the room. I both knew and didn't know the enormity of what had just happened. It would turn out to be entirely life changing for both of us.

He loved my music (I think). He would direct that show or possibly any other shows I wrote in the future (I'm pretty sure). We could go into rehearsal whenever I was finished with the writing. (I remember).

And as I am writing this chapter, nearly fifty years later, I can still capture that moment the music came to life as the God gift that it was. It was an expression of Spirit that had just been birthed.

How did I ever write a musical with no musical training? How did I find the courage to call this unknown person a third time after he turned me down twice? Why did he finally give in? I wouldn't have called him a fourth time! Thoughts and words do not provide answers. God was there.

And in this very moment of writing these words, I realized again that *everything* happened in my dining room, the place where we are fed. My God experience was in the dining room; my piano and all its music "lived" in the dining room. Like many families, we almost never ate in the dining room. It turned out to be God's Room!

It made me smile, touching my spirit with a depth and wonder that only God moments provide.

Unexplainable, but real; mysterious but present! God and Love in action in the center of life

So simple, so uncomplicated, so powerful, so permanent—so Life Giving and life Restoring.

I don't think of God "having a plan for my life". Rather I always think of God as being Present in my life. It is our permanence and grounding in a transitional world that moves us from crisis to crisis; the music and harmony that sustains us and links us to others. It is the source and grounding of love when life loses clarity and meaning. It is God with us, and always gratitude and prayer, praise and peace, hope and love. Amen

CHAPTER 45

Dancing With God

And all of life is made new.

One night, recently, I have a dream. I am in the second floor of a church, not the sanctuary or chapel; not the library or offices; not the Sunday school room but on the second floor where people might meet to talk or eat (the upper room).

The room is quite large, with possible sliding doors to create smaller rooms in this large space. But the current arrangement is just the large room with a few tables and chairs, larger than card tables, but not so large as to be considered as banquet tables. The kitchen is separated by a wall.

There are no table cloths, napkins or silver on the few tables that are standing. The surface of the table is attractive, warm polished wood, with no candles or other decoration. It is ready for use.

This is a large room with many possibilities and purposes for any size group of people. The ceiling is not too high, creating a sense of intimacy even in this large space.

The floor is polished wood, smooth and quite beautiful.

I am waiting, sitting on a chair at one of the tables. There is no one else in the room.

God arrives. He is dressed in a suit, with his tie loosened and the top button on his shirt opened. He is carrying a fairly large brief case which looks rather heavy. He doesn't look tired. On the contrary, he looks quite animated, anticipating our meeting. He looks around and sees me, puts his brief case down on one of the other chairs and walks over to where I am seated.

Without a word, God holds out his arms for us to dance.

I stand and walk into his arms and our dance starts immediately. I don't recognize the music that has started to play. We are in perfect rhythm and connection. The music seems to match our dance perfectly.

We fit, body to body, hands to hands. Our feet move effortlessly together in perfect harmony with each other. We could have danced forever. It was so easy.

We dance for hours—maybe a lifetime. Dancing with God is all there is; no time, no space, no interruptions. The dance is the beginning and the ending and whatever lies in between.

I experience a contentment and peace I've never known before. The dance and God and I are fully connected: each to each with no separation. It is beyond words: a state of two-becoming-one.

The dream doesn't end. Instead the world intervenes. My alarm goes off and I awake.

I am filled with sadness and loss. I can slip back into the dream for another moment or two and touch the reality of my dance with God. But I also know the dance is over. It is time to return to life. However, the dream remains in my spirit and has never left me. I can return to it any time I choose and re-live those moments of complete harmony with God.

It is this dream that prompted the theme of this book. I knew it should be one of the last chapters in the book. But all that preceded this dream, all the gifts of God's Presence in my life, needed to be told first.

We *do fit*, creature and creator. Love is the bond that holds us together. And God, who works hard to keep us together, is the partner who fully enters into the dance we share.

Our dance is ageless, effortless, immediate and intimate. Not sensual, but deeply connected.

We are at one in the dance, fully capable of intricate rhythms and motions because we are so bound to each other.

God as a "business man" indicates God's continued involvement in the world. There is still work to be done. God's gender is not the issue. It could as easily have been a business woman carrying a brief case.

But, clearly God is also willing to release the work to continue the essence of the relationship between us: open, accepting, loving, fulfilling, one-on-one within the harmonies of connection. Even when interrupted, the dance can always begin again in the mutuality of the relationship.

There is an amazing symmetry in my dream and a completion of a long life cycle. In my very early years, dancing was an expression of spirit and energy and a life-line to the future. In my closing years, God becomes my partner in a dance of love and connection: Life fulfilled and complete.

For each of us, there is a dance with God that speaks of our relationship, our time together in harmony and love. For each of us there is an *intimacy* available with God that can be in every moment we discover that God is always right here . . . right now. We are not alone.

Open your heart, open your arms to the always-connecting-God whose mission is to bring you into New Life. Turn up the music, and enter into the dance that leads to knowing God with all your heart, your mind, your body and spirit.

God is as close as the next moment. Let the world with all its demands and urgencies go.

Close your eyes to the interruptions that plague our lives. Take a deep breath to capture this instant of time. Let your heart feel the presence of God in this life-giving moment.

Let all of your being know that God is right here—right now. Nothing can separate you from the knowledge and Love of God for the rest of your life and into eternity. Amen and Amen.

CHAPTER 46

The Final Dance

God at Debbie's Place

Two days ago, when I thought this book was entirely finished and was feeling that sort of "isn't this wonderful to be finished" feeling, my computer stopped working.

If the computer had to break down, it certainly chose a marvelous time. But, in no time, those good feelings were replaced with the reality of the situation. Could I still print this book? Were all those words lost forever? I spent the next day trying to find someone to help after a sleepless night that can only happen when we realize how dependent we are on these electronic machines.

The only comfort I found was in a 4:00 a.m. prayer that said, "God, I know there's a gift hidden in this situation. Help me to find it . . . please."

Today, while waiting for help to come, I used the hours to sort through the notes that went into the writing of this book. And I found the *gift!*

This amazing God of Surprise didn't cause my computer breakdown. I don't ever try to "explain" this God of Mystery and Presence. But my experience of "God at Debbie's Place" had somehow slipped through the cracks of experiences to be shared and simply reappeared when I had the time to look for it.

Another name for God is surely the God of the lost and the found. And, as it turns out, "God at Debbie's Place" is the right experience to share at the end of this book.

Debbie is a waitress at a small, casual restaurant in Canada named, "Let Them Eat Cake". About five feet, four inches tall, small in stature but huge in spirit, Debbie is unforgettable.

She wears a smile that greets you when you walk in the door as if you were the *one* person she wanted to see that day. If you've been there before, you also get a hug that envelopes you with arms that speak the same message. You are welcomed in a way that assures your worth and value. You are special and Debbie lets you know it.

She'll remember exactly what you've eaten before. Coffee or tea appear instantly. Each order is received with a smile and an affirmation that this meal will be prepared exactly to your liking.

When your food arrives, it is delivered with the same loving gesture. You will enjoy this meal and it will be good for you. Your pleasure is her greatest concern.

Her food delivery is a kind of rapid dance as she manoeuvers her way around chairs, tables, and open spaces to reach you as fast as possible with your food selection. All this is accomplished with a smile and non-stop greetings to other customers along the way.

When it is time to leave, Debbie's hug and smile will affirm that you are surely the most important person in her life. Her love will go with you wherever you go until you return to Debbie's Place. You have been thoroughly greeted, fed and loved and each person has been greeted, fed and loved in *exactly* the same way,

You have been nourished and gifted by this generous love that knows no boundaries.

I think God must be a lot like Debbie. Or Debbie is a lot like God. We'd go a long way toward changing this world if we were a lot more like Debbie and God with each other.

Greeting, Feeding, Loving! Debbie makes it look easy. Surprise, New Life, Transformation! God offers us minute by minute opportunities to change our lives and our relationships with other people.

A few years ago at a wedding reception, I stood watching all the young people dancing, mostly the women, thoroughly enjoying themselves. I was envying their spontaneity and their pleasure when a voice behind me said, "Want to dance?"

I turned around to see a very tall, young woman inviting me to dance. I demurred. "I'm too old; I have a bad back; I don't know how to do these modern dances." She simply repeated her invitation with a smile. "Want to dance?"

I found myself still resisting her invitation. I'd look foolish; I've not been on a dance floor in years; and these dances went on endlessly. I looked up at her and her encouraging smile. I thought about God and Surprise and New Life. I hesitated, looked around, took a deep breath and said, "Yes."

God is constantly extending the invitation.

> Do you want to dance?
> Do you want to dance with me?
> Do you want to dance with me right now?

All you have to say is "yes". God is waiting to begin and new life is always ready to surprise us!

YOUR STORY COULD BE THE NEXT CHAPTER IN THIS BOOK!

CHAPTER 47

On Prayer, Gratitude
And Endings

Final Words

I. _PRAYER_ is the language of our relationship with God. It happens in multiple expressions: silent prayer, spoken prayer, prayer in written words. Prayer can also be expressed in non-verbal works of art, music, and literature in their attempts to describe our relationship with God.

Sometimes words interfere with our prayer life when we seek to find the *right* words to use. The mystery and fullness of that amazing relationship transcends most of the words we have available to describe it. Questions about prayer abound: Do I ask for what I need or want to happen? Or does God already know my wants and my needs? Is it selfish to concentrate on myself?

And so we go back to square one. How do we "speak" to God? Does God actually "hear" our prayers? Will God respond to our prayers? What if God is silent?

In the New Testament, we are told to "pray without ceasing". Easier said than done! But an idea worth thinking about. If we pray without ceasing, we are grounding ourselves in prayer, but not necessarily in the everyday activities of life.

Or, putting it another way, if we are to pray without ceasing, we could begin with prayer *and then let life enter into our prayer*. That changes everything!

If I start my day in the grounding experience of having a conversation with God (which is what prayer really is), then it is the base-line, the anchoring and the foundation for the day:

"God, you are the entire reason I am having this conversation with you. So at the beginning of a new day, I am open to whatever the day brings me. Knowing I cannot always determine what a *good* or a *bad* outcome might be when something happens in my life, I will attempt to live this day in both activity and anticipation that you will help me to discover your presence throughout the day.

Help me to see your love manifest in my work and the people I care about. Help me to grow in your love. Amen."

Prayer is conversational. God doesn't seem to require any special language or gesture. In fact, we can get lost in *required words* and step out of the reality we're living.

Praying without ceasing says that God *wants* to have a continual conversation with us to stay connected. Otherwise, why would we be admonished to engage in all day and night prayer?

As we have spent these last twenty years in research about God, we've greatly increased our own prayer lives. We pray before each meal and at the end of the day together. Our prayers are always out loud but generally not repetitious. It has greatly changed our prayer lives to speak our prayers out loud. It also allows prayer to be another activity we share.

It doesn't interfere with my own personal prayers—which are often spoken out loud as well. "God, where are you? I don't understand what's going on. Help!" Or sometimes, "God, I am so grateful. Thank you".

Some people tell me they are very uncomfortable praying out loud: it makes them distressed, uneasy, and restricts the content of their prayers. They just don't want to try it, generally because they don't want the content of their prayers to be judged as acceptable or not. They find a much stronger political *correctness* in praying silently.

Others tell me they're willing to take a chance with spoken prayer. Usually they find it surprisingly meaningful once they've passed through the familiar barriers of what's correct and discover the gift of praying and listening to the prayers of another person.

I have left the world of silent prayer to those few occasions when silence is important or necessary. But I find that my life is always deeply enriched by hearing others pray in their own words about God in their lives.

The real gift of spoken prayer is that it acknowledges the presence of God. I am not having a conversation with myself alone. God and I are in this conversation together. The reality of God in my life is affirmed and acknowledged. God is the gestalt of the experience allowing it to happen.

If you've never tried praying with another person, you have a gift in store. Approach it easily without attempting to predict what will be said. Choose a person you think might be a willing compatriot. Holding hands can be a powerful connecting link without words. Make sure the other person is willing to engage in the intimacy of touch. Ask first.

As you engage in more prayers, with others or alone, God will become even more real in your life. When God is no longer a stranger but someone with whom you have many conversations, you will begin to anticipate prayer as a necessary part of your life.

We pray because we have a direct relationship with God that requires our interaction and our sense of partnership in the living of our lives. We are not looking so much for direct answers as having a dialogue that allows us to reflect and rethink life on a spiritual plane.

In the intimacy of prayer, God becomes a life companion—and a spiritual partner. The language between us grows as we use it, becoming a personal and intimate affirmation of God-Constant in our lives.

Prayer is like any skill. The more we use it, the more often we take it out and try it, the more comfortable it will become and the more necessary it will feel.

My understanding of God is that's exactly what God is looking for also: an intimate experience of conversation in which our relationship becomes the anchor of everything we do. Our lives are brought to God to be shared, loved and healed. Prayer is the language between us.

II. *GRATITUDE* is both part of our prayer lives with God and also the basis for our spiritual growth. We grow in gratitude. Gratitude fills us with spirit. Gratitude helps us to see the world in new and unexpected ways. Discovered gratitude, when we don't feel it at first, is quite miraculous.

In the beginning, we generally link gratitude with the receiving of good *things*. Good results, good experiences, good outcomes in anything we do. It's a philosophy that defines "good" as something that makes us feel happy, satisfied or content. We are truly grateful for all the "good gifts" we have received.

But gratitude is much larger than that limited view. Real gratitude comes when I learn that not all gifts make me feel good. Not all people are happy to be with me. Not everyone agrees with me,

Real gratitude arrives in hard lessons learned and mistakes made. Real gratitude comes when you have hit bottom and learned there actually is a way *up*.

Spirit filled gratitude is hard work. We'd much prefer the kind that makes us feel good. But when we can say, "God I am really grateful ", when it is a learning lesson that has caused me pain and suffering, we know that we are making progress.

It's not that God "wants" us to suffer. Rather, it appears that God is always trying to help us to grow in ways that allow us to see a bigger picture in life.

Gratitude is a powerful and real anchor in the aging process. To look back at my life in disappointment or in sorrow is a deeply painful experience. Gratitude as we grow older is not a choice but a necessity. The opposite of gratitude is despair and the concomitant feelings of loss and sadness.

In recent years, the issue of gratitude has been expressed in many popular versions including the admonition to be *grateful* for at least three items per day as a necessary part of good mental health.

But spiritual gratitude demands much more of us and has far greater benefits.

Spiritual gratitude begins with God and the prayerful conversations we can have with God. It allows us to say to God: I'm working on this issue of Gratitude—I move forward and backward, but I keep at it.

Spiritual gratitude allows us to work toward a time when we can say with conviction, I am really grateful for my life as I have lived it and for the people I've known throughout that life. It allows me to own the hard lessons, the wrong decisions, the hurts I've inflicted on others and the mistakes made. The outcomes in life are part of the mystery in life that I may never fully understand.

It is a curious kind of *confessional* that allows me to own the acceptance of life lived and the *absolution* of knowing that I am continuing to grow.

Gratitude to God for every moment lived is the ultimate gift of life and the measure of our having lived it.

III. *ENDINGS:*

There will always be more to think about, pray about and write about. But ideas and books must come to an ending place.

I am grateful that you have taken the time to read this book or parts of this book.

I hope that some of it has introduced you to God and connected to your life.

I pray that this is just a beginning for you to think about God as a deeply personal *friend* who is also a constant in your life.

I know that God is everywhere, actively engaged in the world, available at any time, to anyone.

I believe we each have an obligation to share our God experiences to enable others to find God in their lives.

Our "Brand", which is a special gift from God, is the best way I know to end this book.

DISCOVER GOD! SHARE THE GIFT!
CHANGE YOUR LIFE! CHANGE THE WORLD!

Amen!

PART V

AFTERWARD: SPECIAL RESOURCES— SPECIAL FRIENDS—SPECIAL PROGRAMS

Fifty years ago, God walked into my life and transformed everything in it:
With a giant broom, God swept the old away, expanding the now—open—space to receive the first gifts of Spirit.

In an instant, it was filled with music, love, and people;
Dreams filling the corners with possibilities reaching up to a non-existing ceiling.
No limits could impede Spirit's journey into life.

Doors opened to receive this burst of new life;
Newly-found-others entered those doors and stayed.
Spirit grew to include all-people-everywhere who could recognize what Spirit was bringing into the world.

Years became more years until everything became One-Happening;
One people; One body of Spirit; One message for All.

God is Real; God is Now. God is With Us. God is Forever.

In Praise-Giving to the God who sweeps the "old" away and opens the world to New Life!

In Thanks-Giving to all who recognized Spirit unfolding and stayed to help.
In Love-Giving to all who have joined us on the journey.

Blessings,
Bobbie McKay
2013

SYNOPSIS OF RESEARCH
PROJECTS AND PROGRAMS

Research Projects and Programs:

1993-1995: The Spiritual Healing Project: Defined; sample selected; endorsed by the United Church of Christ.

1996-2001: Study conducted in protestant (UCC and Episcopal), Catholic, Reform Jewish Congregations.

1999-2000: Presentation and data gathering at the Religious Experience Research Centre, Oxford University, UK.

2001-2002: Interfaith Adolescent Study and Interfaith Military Chaplain Program.

2003-2007: Spiritual Life in the Aging Process: An Interfaith Study.

2004-2008: Quantitative Data archived at CTS, 2004 Adjunct Faculty at CTS 2004, 2005, 2008 intensive classes.

2007-2008: The Meaning of Spiritual Health: An Interfaith Study.

2008-2009: The Prayer Project: Exploring the Mystery of Prayer for those who pray for others.

2009-Ongoing: The Muslim Connection: Spiritual Life in the Islamic Community.

2009-Ongoing: Making the Church a Spiritual Destination: Creating a Spiritual Life Team.

2011-Ongoing: The Interfaith Dialogue: Rochester, N.Y., Cocoa Beach, FL.

2013-New: "Many Faces: An Inter-Spiritual Program for Adolescents and Young Adults.

Data processed at Johns Hopkins University School of Medicine, Center for Learning and Health and partially analyzed at the University of Pennsylvania. Data examined by George Gallup, Jr.

BOOKS AND PUBLICATIONS

Healing the Spirit: Stories of Transformation. Thomas More Press, 2000.

Religion and Healing in America. Oxford University Press, 2005, Chapter 2.

Taking a Chance on God: Exploring God's Presence in our Lives. IUniverse Press, 2007.

When God Becomes Real: Stories of Presence—Models of Church. Exploration Press, 2008.

Dancing with God and Other Stories about God in the World. 2013

"The Spiritual Healing Project", De Numine, The Journal of the Religious Experience Research Centre, Oxford University, UK. 1999.

"The Spiritual Healing Project Goes to School", The Christian Science Sentinel, 2004.

AUTHOR'S CREDENTIALS

Reverend Bobbie McKay, Ph.D. is a graduate of Garrett Theological Seminary and holds Ph.D. in Counseling Psychology from Northwestern University. She is a licensed psychologist and an ordained minister in the United Church of Christ. Dr. McKay has been engaged in both of these helping/healing professions for over forty years. She is the author of four books and co-author of two other books with her husband, Lewis Musil.

Dr. McKay has led over nine hundred seminars and workshops having to do with spiritual and psychological health. Her most recent programs are "Making God Real in Religious and Non-Religious Settings: Building Spiritual Life Teams"; "The Interfaith Dialogue"; and "Many Faces: An Inter-Spiritual Program for Adolescents and Young Adults" with Lew Musil.

Lewis A. Musil holds a Bachelor's Degree from the University of Chicago and a Master of Fine Arts Degree from the Art Institute of Chicago. Mr. Musil is a writer with a background in Media Production. He was also Chairman of the Department of Creative Drama in the Evanston Public Schools.

"TAKING A CHANCE ON GOD" REVEREND BOBBIE MCKAY, PH.D. AND LEW MUSIL MFA

FOREWORD BY GEORGE GALLUP, JR.

"Open your spiritual eyes and say "yes" to God is the passionate and persistent message of this remarkable book. Readers are urged to step aside from their frantic day-to-day existence and recognize the unexpected presence and action of God in their lives.

The authors, Bobbie McKay and Lew Musil, are understandably enthusiastic about conveying this message to readers because they, themselves, have traveled extensively across the country, listening to the heart-gripping and trans-formative spiritual experiences of hundreds of people in all walks of life.

These case histories (and more than 3,000 people were interviewed for the study, which is the basis for this book) are so powerful and compelling that the authors say that they themselves have been transformed by the process. "It was indescribably unexpected journey," they write, "filled with 3,000 surprises and utterly life-changing for us."

TAKING A CHANCE ON GOD is an important, breakthrough book because not only is it based on a huge number of in-depth and personal stories of God's action in human life, but because these interviews form a representative sample (with the correct proportions of various religious and demographic groups) and can thus be projected to the nation as a whole. The study and book fully satisfy the need for both professionally conducted qualitative and quantitative research. The authors have approached this exploration of God's interaction with humans with full objectivity, not imposing and theological or programmatic restrictions on the questions for findings. Their writing represents a clear and lively portrait of the baseline dimensions of spirituality of the U.S. population.

Most of the people they interviewed were ready and eager to share their experiences. "The unexpected and transforming presence of God," the authors write, "is occurring at the present time and is happening to ordinary people." Indeed, readers will find themselves in some of the transforming and liberating experiences recorded.

McKay and Musil have poured their hearts, and minds and souls into this effort. They have a treasure in their hands, and their enthusiasm about the project was apparent when we met together on two occasions at my offices in Princeton, New Jersey, in which we discussed the survey results from the nine-page questionnaire, and their implications for individuals and society as a whole.

Nine out of every 10 people interviewed reported having had at least one experience of spiritual healing that had transformed their lives. The statistical evidence clearly indicates that spiritual healings happen all the time, and to all sorts and conditions of people. The survey data and their own personal experience from a multitude of face-to-face interviews lead the authors to point to a "healing reality in a broken world," and to state boldly, "The question of the existence of God is not a matter of faith, but of statistical reality.

McKay and Musil remind us that the unfilled moment or split second becomes an opportunity to see God. We are to continue to be present and available to God. When we walk with God, we shall not simply _believe_, but _know_. This book is an earnest invitation to readers to say "yes" to God, to be quick to obey spiritual promptings and leadings, and to ask the critical question: Where is God in this moment?

In a concluding chapter, "Take a Chance on God," McKay and Musil offer practical suggestions for entering the nearer presence of God: assume God is present and active, and even if you do not believe this, act as if this is true. Don't look for God in the usual places, keep your heart and mind open—and look for surprises.

Analysis of the findings uncovers certain basic themes in the responses of persons who have had a trans-formative healing experience: they are less self-centered and ego-bound; more open to other people; and have a greater sense of peace in their lives. Having received the gift of God's presence, say these two intrepid explorers of their inner life, McKay and

Musil, one is under obligation to share it. Not to share the gift is to lose it. Healing stories will heal others.

It is exciting to reflect upon the potential that this imposing body of qualitative and quantitative research has for bringing about healing relationships among people at the deepest level. The authors have done the scientific and religious worlds a great service in probing beneath the surface of life to give us new and fresh insight into the action and presence of God in human existence."

George Gallup Jr.
Princeton, New Jersey—2007

THE RELIGIOUS EXPERIENCE RESEARCH CENTRE
WESTMINSTER COLLEGE, OXFORD UK

Peggy Morgan MA
Director

"Reverend Dr. Bobbie McKay and Lewis Musil MA contacted The Religious Experience Research Centre during 1999. They had at that time become aware of its profile and the considerable overlap of focus in the areas of spirituality and religious experience between its work and their own research on Spiritual Healing called *The Spiritual Healing Project*. At the invitation of the Director of RERC and at their own expense, a visit to Oxford and the Religious Experience Research Centre was planned during mid-November 1999. Prior to their visit, Bobbie McKay and Lew Musil wrote an account of their project for the journal of the RERC. This appeared in *De Numine* in September 1999. It provided an excellent briefing for discussions with them in Oxford, describing clearly as it did the range and findings of their research and what they still hope to do. It is obvious that their project is complimentary to the work of the plans to extend their interviewing to members of a variety of faiths, not just those within the denominations of the Christian religion, will make it an interesting and invaluable contribution to our understanding of contemporary spirituality.

Whilst in Oxford Bobbie McKay and Lewis Musil examined accounts relevant to their research in the unique archives of first hand experiences which the Centre holds. They also participated in various seminars in Oxford and were able to be in contact with other interested people in UK. A climax of their visit was a very successful day seminar and discussion with members of the Alister Hardy Society, the friends' organization which supports the work of the Religious Experience Research Centre.

The Religious Experience Research Centre hopes to keep closely in touch with Bobbie and Lew, to use their published work in its education programme and to report to its members, when appropriate, their continuing findings. The Director found not only their efficiency but also their sympathetic style of working an important aspect of their research. It was a pleasure to have face-to-face contact and an ongoing relationship with such able and enterprising researchers."

CENTER FOR THE STUDY OF WORLD RELIGIONS
HARVARD UNIVERSITY

Susan Sered, Ph.D.
Research Director
Religion, Health, and Healing Initiative

"Over the past two years I have had the opportunity to talk with Dr. McKay and Mr. Musil about their Spiritual Healing Project and found them to be unusually widely informed regarding spirituality and healing beliefs in the United States. The breadth of material that they have amassed in their research is truly impressive, and constitutes a unique contribution to the understanding of religion in America. Their book is based on a remarkably large study of the meaning of spiritual healing in mainstream religious congregations.

A chapter devoted to their Spiritual Healing Project will appear in *Religious Healing in America* (Oxford University Press, 2004), a volume which came out of the "Religion, Health and Healing Initiative" at the Harvard University Center for the Study of World Religion.

Dr. McKay and Mr. Musil's latest book is one of a series designed to reach the general public with information from their studies to enable others to use this information in their spiritual lives. They do not suggest easy solutions for the enhancement of one's spiritual life. Rather, they invite the reader to share a point of view derived from the study, which may open the door to new ways of looking at the world through "spiritual eyes."

Their writing is cogent and accessible, and should appeal to both lay audiences as well as to clergy and chaplains of a wide range of denominations. The authors include anecdotal stories from many of the participants in their studies. They also share the impact of the Spiritual Healing Project on their own lives in moving and powerful ways making their writing not only readable but compelling in its message of God Present and Active in the world."

REVIEW OF "HEALING THE SPIRIT STORIES OF TRANSFORMATION"

Reverend Stephen Parsons.
Church of England, UK

"Healing the Spirit" is a remarkable book. It presents the fruits of many months of work recording the stories of ordinary people who were asked to react to the phrase, 'spiritual healing.' It communicates vividly the hopes, the joys and the experiences of many people who were enabled by Bobbie and Lew to speak of things in their personal lives that they had never shared before. There was never any attempt by the authors to dictate or manipulate the words and the concepts used. There is thus freshness in the narrative which formal theological writing seldom captures.

The book is based on interviews with members of 101 churches, mainly associated with the United Church of Christ in the States. Later the project was extended to encompass a number of Jewish Synagogues and Catholic Congregations. The language of all participants had much in common and it was as though the language, which communicated the meaning of 'spiritual healing', crossed both denominational and interfaith boundaries.

The authors capture well the creativity shown by individuals who seem to have found enormous liberation and freedom when speaking about experiences that had changed them at every level of their being. It was as though Bobbie and Lew were the catalyst for tapping an enormously rich vein of treasure from the depths of the individual spirit.

One feels deeply privileged to be able to hear such moving testimony in the area of people's personal lives. This is a book that reminds all of us of the profound personal stories that lie within individual lives of ordinary people. It is also fascinating to hear the richness of the words that are used to articulate the deepest things within the individual experiences.

The range of stories is not just about miraculous transformation but also cover accounts of personal struggles to overcome setbacks on the journey of life. The common theme is that all of them are recounted against the background of a God who is never far away and who enables the possibility of meeting creatively and transforming the trials that are met in the journey of life.

"Healing the Spirit" presents us with a living dynamic theology, which will resonate with the reader in a way, that one feels all good preaching should do, but seldom does. It is an account of experience that evokes in the reader a sense that at the heart of what is truly real in our lives, God is to be found whether in the pain, the loss, or the discovery of joy.

A heart-warming and transformative book that hints to us of a theology that transcends denominational and cultural barriers joining the raw material of human experience to the capacity of the divine to transfigure and make New."

REVEREND DR. FRED FOURIE, PASTOR, COCOA BEACH COMMUNITY CHURCH

Cocoa Beach, Florida:

"When Dr. McKay approached me with the possibility of creating a spiritual life team at Cocoa Beach Community Church, as part of her program to make the church a spiritual destination, it seemed like a reasonable idea and a good thing to do.

However, I had no idea of what a powerful program it would become. It has not only transformed the team members themselves, but it has opened the whole issue of spiritual life into the congregation as well.

When the spiritual life team spent two consecutive Saturday mornings sharing their spiritual experiences with the congregation, it became clear that the whole church was in the process of becoming a spiritual destination.

The movement of the team into the community at large through contact with other denominational leaders and congregations is something I would never have predicted as a possibility.

But it has become a fact here in Cocoa Beach. Other denominations are welcoming the opportunity for our Spiritual Life team to share their experiences and what it has meant in their lives as a way to help build new teams in their congregations and increase the spiritual connections between us. It also opens the door to spiritual solutions for shared community problems.

In my ministry, the opportunity to be a member of the spiritual life team has enriched my spiritual connections both to the team and to the congregation.

The power of this simple act of sharing spiritual experiences is amazing both in its simplicity and in its power to transform the church.

I cannot overstate the possibilities of this program to truly make the church a spiritual destination for all people."

The Reverend Jay Sidebotham, Rector, The Church of the Holy Spirit,

Lake Forest, Illinois

"It has been my joy and privilege to come to know Bobbie McKay and Lew Musil. They have been called to a powerful ministry: helping people to tell their own stories of God at work in their lives. Bobbie and Lew have recognized that the needs for healing surround us, and that God's power is at work bringing wholeness where there is brokenness. They bring open heats, keen minds, boundless energy and deep faith to their exploration. I heartily recommend them to those hoping to strike up a conversation about the marvel and mystery of God at work in our world. You'll be blessed by their presence."

The Reverend Gilbert W. Bowen, Retired Pastor

"A remarkable study: Bobbie and Lew have created a work of faith and love, yet objectivity and openness, in which they have surfaced experiences of spiritual healing in the lives of people within the mainstream church and synagogue. What is amazing is the growth that has been going on unrecognized by the religious establishment, and even avoided as culturally taboo or creedally dangerous. But the Spirit clearly blows where it will and their research clearly demonstrates this reality. Here is a real breakthrough that deserves the attention of clergy and people of faith."

John Shea, Author, Lecturer, Story Teller

"Knowing is not an act of stepping back, but stepping into. It is not an act of disengagement, but of communion. I remembered this teaching when I read the personal and engaged way Bobbie and Lew went about trying to understand spiritual healing in the lives of people. Bobbie began with her own experience and asked if it resonated with anyone else. Most of the world raised their hands. Their storytelling sessions became a community of people listening to one another and entering into each other's experience. Listen with openness to their stories, allowing this listening to spur your own memory and recall your own experiences, and tell them to a friend. If you do this, you will have an intuitive sense of what spiritual healing is—and you may be surprised that you are no stranger to it."

Reverend Gregory Sakowicz
Catholic Archdiocese of Chicago, IL

"We all somehow seek to connect the mystery of God with the mystery of our lives . . . HEALING THE SPIRIT IS OUR STORY. Reverend McKay and Lewis Musil beautifully thread our stories with the Spirit of God as the master weaver. For life is a mystery to be lived and not a problem to be solved."

Rabbi Douglas Kohn
San Bernardino, Ca.

"Thank you for sharing the Spiritual Healing Project with members of Beth Tikvah Congregation. We deeply appreciate your candor, genuine interest and kindness, and your willingness to share your work with us. As much as you gained from our group, you gave so very much more. Thank you. We would be more than willing to provide references to our colleagues, lay and professional, to help you bring the Project to other synagogues."

THE REVEREND PAUL SHERRY, PH.D., FORMER PRESIDENT, UNITED CHURCH OF CHRIST.

"Healing the Spirit is a book of transformation. It speaks with grace, integrity, power and joy to the spiritual healing that accompanies the awakening sense of God's presence in all our lives. The personal stories of spiritual healing of so many people from so many differing backgrounds and places are both moving and renewing. To read these stories is to have one's own spirit healed. That certainly was true for me and I am sure will be true for many others as well."

REVEREND ELIZABETH ANDREWS PRESBYTERIAN MINISTER AND SPIRITUAL DIRECTOR

"This remarkable, faithful couple has been on a Spirit-led journey, and they share with us wonderful gifts gathered in the process: stories of God's presence or action in people's lives, moments of transformation, and a vocabulary for us to use in speaking of these experiences to one another. Graced intersections of the ordinary and the eternal abound, and there is power in naming them aloud in the presence of others. How amazing, how liberating, how fitting, if our churches could once again become 'safe places' where these experiences can be told and validated!"

THE REVEREND WENDY LANE, RETIRED EPISCOPAL PRIEST

"Awesome is the word that comes to mind . . . I am a priest and it was the very first time I had ever told my own story of Spiritual Healing. Bobbie and Lew gave me and others a safe and holy space in which to give voice to our faith in the healing power of God."

T. Tolbert Chisum,
Businessman and Philanthropist

"Dr. Bobbie McKay and Lewis Musil have uncovered God's secrets and blessed joy in their quest to find the truth about the healing spirit. Neither gender, race, education, religion, nor position can stop God's grace for all mankind. Travel with Bobbie and Lew as they witness their incredible journey into the churches, temples and synagogues and come face to face with the healing spirit."

The Reverend Jane Fisler Hoffman,
Former Illoinois Conference Minister
Of The United Church Of Christ

"The Spiritual Healing Project brings good news to the United Church of Christ: there is spiritual hunger and there are experiences of spiritual healing among our faith family AND they are not defined or bound by anyone else's narrow definitions. I think this project invites the United Church of Christ into our deepest and more urgent evangelical frontier: the explicit sharing of our faith story."

Excerpts from "The Spiritual Healing Project
Goes to School", The Christian Science Sentinel,
September 12, 2004.

"Following their visit with Sentinel editors in Boston (see the July 19-26 issue, "The rise of spiritual healing," pages 8-13, or go to www.cssentinel. com), spiritual healing researchers Bobbie McKay and her husband, Lewis Musil, returned home to prepare to teach a one-week course called "Spirituality and Healing" at the Chicago Theological Seminary. We asked Dr. McKay to let us know how the course went, and here's her account of what one seminarian called "a life-changing experience.""

"Each day we shared stories, theirs and ours. Daily, we prayed four times together-at the beginning of class, before lunch, and at the beginning and end of the afternoon session. After the first day, class volunteers provided the prayers, which grew in meaning and power. It became very comfortable to pray four times a day in community, hands linked, hearts and spirits breathing in the presence of God."

"We shared all that we had learned from our Spiritual Healing and Spiritual Aging Projects, and how our lives had been transformed by meeting with over 3,000 people from many different congregations. We spoke of ways in which the seminarians, as future clergy, could utilize our findings in their ministries and their lives. We looked at issues of clergy burnout, at the problems they would most likely encounter in their churches as clergy, and at the struggles of clergy families."

"We laughed a lot, cried together, and spoke of life lived-all of which meant speaking about God. We shared meals, coffee, hugs, love, moments of music, and the depth of silence. We learned from each other, and from God, the highest form of learning. We watched the personal and the professional become joined together into one spiritual whole."

The final gift from the class was their words written on cards for us:

"Thank you for the joy, the laughter, and the tears. The Healing and Spirituality Project is a blessing to my soul."

"You have given us energy and vision." "Thank you for helping really bring the Spirit into CTS!"

"Thank you for this opportunity this week. It's been a spiritual healing just being here."

"Thank you for sharing your gifts and releasing the gifts within us. This has been a life-changing experience for my mind. The best is yet to come through the Holy Spirit Thank you for being open enough to share."

STUDENT EVALUATIONS FOR COURSES TAUGHT AT
CHICAGO THEOLOGICAL SEMINARY

"This class . . ." Clearly defined the role of Spirituality in ministry. I felt for the first time in Seminary that I had an understanding of my call and the call of others."

"Their project on Spirituality and teaching has provided me with more preparation for ministry than any other class."

"The instructors were excellent, a team working in the Spirit as one to the Glory of God. The example of their shared ministry was phenomenal."

"This class . . . provided practical strategies for finding God for ourselves and helping others find God in everyday experiences."

"This class prepared me to think in new ways, challenge myself more and how to choose words carefully. How to see the presence of God in everything."

"All seminary students NEED this class. It was crucial, invaluable and possibly could be the most important course I might ever take."

GOD AND THE SPIRITUAL LIFE TEAMS

What's in a Team?

Spiritual Life Teams are grounded in the conclusions from our research project:

> God is *real* and available 24/7 for everyone: no exclusions, no exceptions.
> God is like a non-judgmental *change agent* bringing *new life* into present time.
> Surprise is God's signature in the world.

Shared God experiences, prayer and action set the stage for people to look for God experiences in their own lives and become a part of a Spiritual Life Team. A Workbook and Leader's Guide make the process readily accessible: "Making God Real in Religious Settings: Building Spiritual Life Teams; and "Making God Real in Non-Religious Settings: Building Spiritual Life Teams. (Both are available through our website, www.spiritualhealthcenter.org.)

Already successfully tested, this program offers a unique opportunity for people to discover their spiritual lives and engage in life changing, spiritual connections, prayer and actions with others.

Each team is different and autonomous. But they all have the same agenda and final destination: to make God *real* in life. When multiple teams exist in a single setting, they deeply enrich their experience by having periodic *All Teams* meetings in which people experience face to face contact in a larger setting, creating a powerful spiritual energy that is life-giving and life-saving.

The experience of being part of a Spiritual Life Team is both unique and collaborative. The process differs for each person but includes many common themes.

Initial Questions: This feels strange and different from other experiences I've had.—*Uncertainty:* I'm not sure why I'm here.—*Praying out loud?* I've never done this before with other people. What will they think of my prayer?—*Laughter:* This is easier than I thought! Why did it seem so hard?

-*Tears:* My heart is touched by what's happening to me and what I'm hearing from others.—*Discovery:* Hearing someone else talk about God makes me think of a God experience I've had.—*Surprise:* I've never shared a God experience before. It never felt safe. This is different.—*Anticipation:* This is the one meeting I never miss.—*Connection with others:* My team is different from any other group.

-*Amazement:* I am totally amazed that such a simple process is such a deep experience.—*Trust:* I feel I can trust everyone on the team to validate my God experiences and my prayers.—*Reality:* God is becoming *real* in my life.-*Power:* When all our teams meet together, I can feel the power of each of our shared prayers and the power of all our teams being together in one place.—*Love:* is the bond we share with each other and others, the grounding of our experience.

In the experience of being a Spiritual Life Team, God is always present.

Spiritual Life Teams introduce multiple opportunities for people to learn about God; exciting challenges to congregations to bring Spiritual Life into the everyday life of the congregation and to create new spiritual connections to the community at large. Spiritual Life Teams are *good* for congregations and communities.

GOD AND THE INTERFAITH
DIALOGUE PROGRAM

When different faith traditions come together
to talk about God, Peace becomes possible.

This special program brings people of different religious traditions together to discover our common spiritual connections, while retaining our important religious differences. The result is an interfaith community and dialogue that transforms everyone's life in the process.

Too many of our interfaith experiences concentrate on *resolving* our differences or they become attempts to persuade and convince others of the *rightness* of our particular tradition.

This Interfaith Dialogue begins with the *gift* of our differences and advances us to the opportunity of sharing our common God experiences as the denominator of possibilities for interfaith understanding, appreciation and connection.

At this time, the Interfaith Dialogue includes representatives from the four major Abrahamic traditions who meet to pray together and share their God experiences in an environment that is non-political; non-theological and non-confrontive in nature.

These a-political experiences offer the opportunity to discover our spiritual commonalities and the many ways we can unite within those spiritual connections in promoting healing strategies for our lives, our families and our communities.

The Interfaith Dialogue Program has already been successfully tested both in Florida and New York State. The results have been astonishing and highly spiritual in nature. Relying on our common spiritual heritage and treasuring our spiritual differences has allowed us to *meet* in the midst of life and discover God—with—all of us.

The result is a new understanding of the amazing spiritual connections between us and a deepened appreciation of the uniqueness of each of our traditions.

Opening the door to *other* spiritual traditions is our next step in this program to create a larger circle of opportunities to discover our common connections and create strategies for further dialogue in an inter-spiritual community.

In today's very fractured world, there is no more urgent agenda than the discovery of our common spiritual voices and the potential they carry for healing dialogue, understanding and action.

"MANY FACES" AN INTERSPIRITUAL-PROGRAM FOR ADOLESCENTS & YOUNG ADULTS.

*Bringing God into lives on the edge of adulthood
in a changing world!*

This brand new program brings the excitement of the "Interfaith Dialogue" into direct *actions* aimed at restoring spiritual dialogue and peace among all religious groups. It focuses on those nearing adulthood as the group most likely to be seriously engaged in a peace process to change the animosities and hate that are everywhere in our struggling world.

These dedicated young people are not willing to settle for a world in dispute.

They are much more focused on what individuals, working collectively, can accomplish in the way of bringing change and peace into the world.

Their powerful honesty and integrity; their unwillingness to avoid these issues are catalytic in bringing these young adults together.

They will not settle for a world of dishonesty and distrust. They look for people to demonstrate their willingness to help and to model what can be done to change the destructive course the world seems to be following.

Comfortable in a spiritual environment that is honest, where actions match words, and where people are willing to share their questions, doubts and concerns, these young people will engage in a spiritual inquiry and discussion that listens to all viewpoints.

Their spiritual energy is waiting to be gathered and expressed. The opportunity for our participation in their spiritual path, at their level of honesty, is a gift we dare not lose. Their ability to reach out electronically to their peers around the world makes this program a world-wide reality.

"Many Faces" brings *one spirit* into the world to change the world!

**George Gallup, Jr. and Dr. Bobbie McKay,
Princeton, New Jersey, 2011**